Our Youth Speak, Will We Listen?

Our Youth Speak, Will We Listen?

Eric E Smith, Editor

EDG Learning Press
2015

First Printing: 2015

ISBN 978-0-9833701-2-3

EDG Learning Press
6482 S Beech Cir #437
Littleton, CO 80127

press.edglearning.com

Contents

Preface

Our youth speak, will we listen?

It's not "can we listen," not "could we listen," not even "should we listen." All of those let us passively dismiss the opportunity. But "will we listen" asks us to be active in making the choice to listen. And that choice requires making a second choice, "What do I do with what I have heard, learned?" That is the choice we want you to "have" to make.

Where did the idea for putting you, our reader, in the position of making the choice come from? Why do we want to do that? It would be so much easier to leave the world to its own devices, for good or ill. To understand the genesis of this book, I have to share a small part of my back-story, not enough to be maudlin, just enough to see the genesis of our passion.

It was a mid-life crisis, though not your typical "I'm 50 and I don't want to get old," crazy crisis. It was brought on by a number of large changes in my life, which caused me to ask, "What do I want to be when I grow up?" It wasn't so much about growing up, as it was about my mission, my calling in life, now that things were different. It is a question we all face when our world changes in significant ways. My specific changes don't really matter, only that they required reflection and a new direction for my life.

What I discovered was that I had been my most fulfilled when I was a graduate student and a swim coach (which paid for graduate school). Why? I was immersed in my studies and I was teaching other, like-minded, academic seekers of truth. More importantly, I was working with young people as a mentor in addition to coach. Being a mentor is a two-way relationship in which the mentor often gains more than the mentee. The young people I spent my time with were teaching me and challenging me to become more than I was, while they strove to become the best they could be, with my help.

So, I became a teacher. Most of the time, I didn't have a classroom full of students who may or may not have wanted to be there. Instead, I was a homebound teacher, working with young people who for medical reasons were unable to attend regular school. I went to them. The goal was to provide education services at the same time they were battling their health issues. What I found is young people who wanted to succeed in spite of difficult, often overwhelming, circumstances. All of the students I worked with recognized that they had extra challenges and still they sought to learn and grow. By approaching their education as a coach, rather than a presenter, I was able to help them set goals and support the process. And, I learned from them.

About this time, my mother passed away. It was a challenge for my whole family. In talking and sharing memories, a picture of my mother's great passion for our youth emerged. She believed, so strongly, our youth are far more capable than society thinks that her passion was transmitted to all of her children. Indeed, all of her children, in one way or another, continue to work with youth.

But what to do with that passion? Through my teaching and my involvement with Scouting, I had encountered a number of young people who loved to write and had exceptional insights. I thought that perhaps their writing could be collected and shared with a wider audience through a book. But, there I was stuck. How would I contact enough writers and obtain their work? While wrestling with the issue, I encountered some young people who really wanted to explore being a writer. They wanted to do more than write papers for school. You might say they were driven by their own passions to write. But they were frustrated - how could they explore their passion and share their insights? The school system wasn't designed to support that kind of exploration. A couple of these young people had been my students, another a Scout. And, they had friends. So in September of 2012, I started a peer critique writers group for high school age young people.

There were five at the first meeting. Over the next few months, they learned how to help each other (and me) improve their writing. We explored techniques and styles. We helped each other with academic papers. There were no restrictions on what we wrote. The only requirement was that we wrote, shared, and provided honest feedback and assistance. My role, initially, was that of facilitator. They named themselves The Writers of the Round Table. We created a web site to support our sharing. Over time, they insisted that I write, too, as a member. And, they inspired me to write in ways other than academic and technical.

At some point during our first year, I realized that I did not need to search for young authors for the book. They were right there, with me. They were already sharing their work. All I had to do was share my dream of giving them a Voice. Thus, this book was born. As with my belief in our young people, it became far more than I had dreamed. It has been a true collaboration. The Writers have been involved in all aspects of this book.

It is my honor and pleasure to present to you the thoughts and dreams of some of our youth. May you gain even a small percent of what they have given me.

Eric E Smith
A Writer of the Round Table
October 6, 2014

A Challenge

Eric Smith

One Sunday morning during Lent, my pastor asked a question of the congregation, “If you could ask Christ anything, what would you ask?” The congregation responded as they thought the pastor wanted – why do bad things happen and so on. It was what one would expect from adults both reflecting on their beliefs and trying to impress others listening.

After a few minutes of sharing, one small boy, about four, raised his hand. The pastor said “George what would you ask?”

George responded “Would you play with me?”

The congregation was silent for a moment. Then a few soft snickers could be heard. Others quietly gasped. No one wanted to hurt George's feelings. But the pastor went further, asking George why that was his question. George responded that he wanted to be friends.

Being friends with God... It is an enormous, yet simple concept. Regardless of your faith, your religion, all of us would like a positive relationship with our Creator, our God. Yet, it took a child to remind us that the important thing is the quality of our relationship. And that was the point the pastor was trying to make in his sermon that day. He followed George's simple statement with a discussion of why it was important. Some in the congregation remarked later that, in the moment, George had shown remarkable wisdom. That wasn't what they really meant, but they didn't want to say, “how dare he be funny in church.”

The incident stuck with me. Over the years, I have reflected on the example of unexpected wisdom in our youth. It really isn't unusual. All of us have experienced and been surprised by the insight of our youth. Frequently, we make some exclamation praising young people even saying (or at least thinking) they are “wise beyond their years.” Indeed, we often tell them they have remarkable insight "for one so young." Then we discount that insight, thinking they are too innocent, too inexperienced for any real insight.

Is that casual dismissal fair?

Consider our fascination with new, young "stars" in sports and entertainment. We watch them, we celebrate their success. We soak up their downfall, using it as a warning to our own children. Then we celebrate when they make a come-back. Sometimes those young people try to make a difference, to share some of their thoughts. But because they are young celebrities, we think that perhaps it really is their PR machine, not the celebrities themselves, that are scripting their lives and statements or examples. And do we listen?

Once in a while a young "star" breaks through, often after personal challenges. And we begin to take her or him more seriously. After-all, they are role models, whether or not they want to be such. And that only increases the pressure and watchfulness we put on them as well as the commentary around and about them. As a result, their messages often are lost in the "noise" that accompanies celebrity. When we do reach through the noise, we often find that the things they are telling us - the challenges they face and the things they have learned - are not much different from what the "ordinary" young people around us are telling us, if we would only listen.

When celebrities do speak out on issues and we can filter out all the noise, they are worth listening to and responding. Perhaps that is why young celebrities are sometimes sought to speak to social issues that impact our youth. Still, it can be a lot of work to find the gems in the media.

These breakthrough celebrities are no more insightful than "ordinary" young people, the youth in our homes, our schools, our communities. Yet we usually pass our youth off before we can really listen to them. Fame and celebrity don't confer wisdom and neither, necessarily, does age. Rather than allowing our youth to go unheard, losing their insights, it is time to listen!

This book is a first step in listening to our youth. It is a collection of writings from a group of young people. It is not exhaustive, nor is it truly representative of all that our youth have to say to each other and to us, the readers. But we have to start somewhere. In this book, you will not find the noise that surrounds our celebrities. Instead, you will find the honesty of our youth, not yet jaded by age and experience.

In the pages that follow, you will encounter a number of young people between the ages of 14 and 19. They are not famous. Even within their own communities they are often invisible. But they are willing to share with us the things all young people face, each with her or his individual take. Will you listen to their voices? More importantly, will you do something positive with what you learn?

You will experience essays, some very personal, poetry and even a short story or two. And you will encounter commentary by the young people who wrote them. You will also find commentary by adults with experience working and listening to our youth.

The writings were collected and then placed into categories, in consultation with the young authors. As the project developed, some gaps were encountered and the authors were asked to contribute additional work they might want in those categories that had few pieces.

Once collected, the authors were asked to contribute commentary. They could comment on their own works or those of other young writers. Then the adults were asked to provide commentary, with at least one adult for each category.

Our challenge to you, our reader, is to listen, reflect, and then do something positive with what you learn.

Bullying

Bullying. It seems to be in the news constantly these days. There is a shooting at a school or place of work and the perpetrator is caught or more often killed (sometimes by his own hand). We learn that he was a victim of bullying. A survey finds that students who have been bullied are more likely to sneak a weapon into school.

So we listen to the "experts." And we set up "no tolerance" policies. Yet the bullying continues and seems to get worse.

A young lady or man in middle or high school commits suicide and we learn he or she was a victim of bullying. We agree that it is sad and something must be done. But what? We try slogans, assemblies, small group discussions and more, but it continues.

Perhaps we should start by listening to young people who have been and are being bullied...

- Eric Smith

War in the School Yard

Rhiannin

It isn't an easy thing to relate the trials of war, the horrors of those experiences, to the life of a seventeen year-old civilian such as myself. I've seen no battlefields, crossed no trenches. I've never fired a gun in the hope that I wouldn't receive a bullet in return. I've never watched my friends die all around me, forced to accept their deaths, and to continue on. I've never been through a world war, or a war of any kind. Not in the conventional sense.

There is only one thing in my life that can be compared, bullying. An obvious example, but it is unfortunately also the very best I have to offer. Bullying in my life is the event, and it has occurred over and over, time and again, throughout my life, the shells that burst amid the trenches of war.

Growing up isn't easy. Anyone who has bothered to do so knows that, and knows that it is marked with periods of difficulty and pain. Bullying is a long standing and largely *accepted* part of growing up. Every child faces at some point or another an instance of name-calling, a rumor, something. For me bullying was much more than that, and was more than occasional.

I've never been normal. I suppose that was obvious to everyone else, though when I was very little I didn't realize that I was quite so strange. Long hair, naturally intense curiosity, and the sort of recklessness that is better and more often associated with young boys made me stand out. Standing-out isn't suggested when growing up. Even in preschool I was easily identified as different. Being different was enough to separate me from them. I wasn't a part of the collective *us* of the other kids.

Looking back I suppose I did know I was different from the other girls, or at least I was conscious of the physical aspects of my difference. The fact that I had long hair and unpainted nails I knew, I never even considered that less obvious things, like wanting to learn to read, could be a part of the separation between them and me. The result was an unofficial 'club'. I say unofficial only because at the preschool level 'clubs' weren't known to the teachers, and really only loosely qualified for the name. The I hate Rhiannin 'club' was what they told me it was called, but in all reality it was just a separation of *us* and *them,* or, in this case, *her.* It being preschool, I remember that the separation was a known one, but not terribly distinct. I liked playing by myself anyway, and it wasn't as if the other kids would outright refuse to play with me; they couldn't without getting in trouble. It was just that they weren't happy about me, and we (the other kids and myself) didn't particularly understand each other. I understood that I didn't have painted nails, they understood that they did.

I wouldn't mention this, except that I can never tell whether this was a nothing event, or the most important. At the time, I remember, it was hard for me to deal with being different. I still don't like seeing the familiar shape of that particular preschool, even though I know that not one of the buildings I've seen in the years since preschool has been the one I actually attended. I remember wondering why they didn't like me. Being convinced that the length of my hair, the plainness of my nails couldn't be it, but having no other explanation, I was forced to attribute the difference to those things, for a simple lack of anything else to blame.

Here was the beginning of my personal war. Here I was entrenched, staring across a field of personal differences. My personal field of battle was a small one, merely the space of a school, and our personal differences were only so big, only so small, as a difference in uniform. But what was beginning was much bigger than that, much bigger than the where's, the why's, the how's.

By the time I was in kindergarten, I was more resigned to not fitting in. I still hadn't accepted that I was different, but I was prepared for the results of it. I was right, I didn't make many friends. This time though, it was even harder to define the differences between myself and my classmates. There were other girls with long hair, other girls with plain nails, the physical differences between me and my classmates were fewer, but the separation was still there, still distinct.

Kindergarten passed quickly. By first grade the teachers cared less about our unity, and, by extension, our dis-unity. So long as they didn't see evidence of the petty rivalries and fighting, they didn't try to prevent it. Recess became an enduring question not of *if* something would happen, but rather *when* and to *whom*. The older kids, now that we were no longer under the protective shadow of a teacher, saw us as easy targets for their own frustrations, and we in turn took those angers out among ourselves.

No one in any grade ever complained about what was going on. As a school, we felt the obligation to at least give an appearance of social unity to our teachers. They were proud of the school, and we were firm in believing that nothing we said would change that. The teachers, the administration, they didn't see it, couldn't see it. They didn't want to. And, none of us was willing to break the illusion. School spirit was a part of the code. We were supposed to be proud of being Wildcats. No one that hadn't seen the reality of school life would have understood why we weren't.

The *us and them* dynamic changed some as we went through the school year. We were united despite our petty dislikes, united against they that were our chief tormentors, the older kids, specifically the sixth grade. On a good day any of us might step in for any other in defense against their attacks. On a bad day we might watch and later console, secretly grateful that we weren't the victim.

We never considered that it might be different, or that we could make it different. No one bothered to listen to the infrequent speeches about what to do in the case of a bully. Telling a teacher made you a target, walking away only made them more determined, none of the little lines we were told succeeded in doing anything but getting us laughed at. Sometimes someone would fight it, would respond with a name, shove back, laugh, yell. These were the only times the teachers ever saw anything, and all it meant was another lecture. No one ever said anything when the person that got in trouble wasn't the one that had started it.

I can't say for any of the others what impact the culture of the school had on them. For me, personally, I ceased to even believe that it could be different, there or anywhere else.

By second grade we were almost numb to it. Not yet old enough to be dealing out cruelties of our own, but too old to be shocked and surprised when someone dealt one to us. It began to be a rare day that someone was overly upset by someone else. We learned to take what was coming, accept it. Just like everyone else.

My best friend at the time, lets call her Amy, was destined to join the ranks of our older tormentors. We all knew it, to some degree or another, but because she was still part of *us* and not yet a part of *them* no one minded much. As her best friend, and thus the person that spent the most time with her, Amy's main practice target was me.

It might be unkind of me to say this, but she wasn't the brightest. Verbal taunting almost completely eluded her. So, rather than verbal taunts, she employed physical strength.

Amy was quick to inform anyone, with a swift punch to the gut, if you had done something she didn't approve of. Almost nothing met with her approval, so we all learned how to shift so that it didn't hurt much. Sometimes she'd catch us unaware though, for doing something she couldn't, saying something she didn't want us to, or hadn't thought of. Even doing well in class could bring retribution.

But Amy wasn't as bad as the fourth, fifth, and sixth graders. From them we all expected to be shoved, mocked, excluded. If a teacher saw you fall, you said you'd 'tripped' or else risked further wrath. If they over-heard name calling, you agreed when they said they were just messing around. If an adult forced a group to let you participate, you did whatever was least obtrusive, and you did it quietly. Telling, complaining, even giving the slightest hint that something was wrong came with a worsening of the issue.

Rumors began to spread when people started standing up for themselves, or others. The first rumors ever told about me were started because I stood up for one of my close friends, Michelle. One of the sixth graders was making fun of her height. Michelle was short. Very short. So, ironically, was the sixth grader. In one of those moments of childish alacrity, I pointed out that he was short too, without considering what would happen. Michelle and I held our breath as we waited for his response. Rather than saying anything just then, he walked away. We couldn't believe our luck. Days later, I realized that the rumors I was just beginning to hear, that many of the people in my class already knew and believed, had been started by that boy, that very day.

Bullying is an insidious thing. It seeps into you, becomes a part of you. The more you are exposed, the better you get at building walls against it, but the more you are exposed, the more brittle those walls become. Eventually something will break through, demolishing all you had built to protect yourself, clawing at all you'd sought to protect.

By the time I'd left second grade in Chicago, moving to Colorado, I'd reached the breaking point. I believed what others told me. I couldn't fight against it. I refused to fight back, thinking that maybe if I accepted it, took what was coming to me uncomplaining, then maybe I'd be better someday than I was then.

When I arrived at my new school I was totally unprepared for the difference. I dreaded being the new kid, hoped my new classmates would just leave me alone. I didn't really want to go to school anymore, despite enjoying learning. I was scared that I'd be too smart, or too dumb, that somehow I'd make myself a target on my first day. Somehow there was a part of me that still hoped, hoped that maybe it would be different at my new school.

It was. The kids were nicer, the teachers more aware, and there were fewer of us. It was harder to go unnoticed. But I didn't trust it. I couldn't. For two years almost nothing went wrong, but still I was wary. I kept to a small group of friends, and didn't really get to know anyone else, or let them get to know me. My fear made me vulnerable to the very thing I was still defending against.

When it started it was mild in comparison, but the part of me that bullying had already infected rose up, whispering its darkness in my ear every time something happened.

Nothing physical ever happened at this school. But rumors began to fly, and one group set out to make a fool of me. Not out of any particular malice, but because I was vulnerable, and they could. Eventually I caught on to what was going on, but not before they'd succeeded in separating me from my real friends. I spent the next year repairing the damage to my friendships, and my reputation.

Bullying didn't end in elementary school. It didn't end in middle school. It hasn't ended in high school. I still expect it, I still wait for it. It still happens, and it still hurts. I avoid certain types of people because of my past, even if I know that as an individual they wouldn't do anything of the sort I expect. I don't relate very well with the majority of people my age, I can't, I never had practice.

Largely my fight with bullying is over. I've finally come to the point where it doesn't matter in the way it used to. It continues to, and always will, hurt. Yet, my part in the fight is done with, in a year's time I will be gone from high school. I will enter the world as the person my experiences have made me. Yet, it's impossible not to wonder who that person would have been, if she'd never had a part in the school yard war.

Potential

George

Potential is something everyone has. Potential means "capable of being or becoming." A student in 3rd grade doing 5th grade math at home with his dad has potential. You cannot take potential from anyone; you can only hinder that person's opportunity to act on it. A broken school system in a small town can strip a child of his or her dreams because their opportunities are hindered.

People are all born with immense potential. But most get their opportunities taken from them whether or not they choose to have them taken. If you have something you want to do or something unfinished and after you pay your dues and somebody says no, who has the right to tell you that? Nobody! Unfortunately it happens every day. Children with a learning disability or disease they cannot control are denied the opportunity to live their dream because of others' ignorance.

Children in this country are constantly taught how to win, but not how to play the game. Teachers are being taught to be a subject matter expert; when they should be taught how to teach. When I say teach I mean, "be able to teach anything to anybody, regardless of disability." Everyone has a disability of some kind, some are just more serious than others. So we decide to penalize people for something they cannot control in an ignorant effort to stop it. Ignorance is the worst disease of the modern world. It will kill thousands every day and kill millions every year without even knowing.

School counselors are a good example. They have an excuse for all your problems and have no solutions for any of them. Everybody "understands," but nobody knows how to help. They tell you to work harder when you're already carrying a burden bigger than any adult or student in that school. But you are always expected to work harder. They smile from their office chair and tell you they are there for you. But are they really? When you bring a real issue about a failing school and staff, what do they do? Look at you and say, "it's your fault and there's nothing anyone but you can do." So you ask, "what can I do?" They simply tell you, "work harder."

People are dumb, stupid, arrogant, mean, selfish, pessimistic, but most of all ignorant. Let me tell you that ignorance or purposeful ignorance to get out of your duties hurts people like me and thousands of others the most. Now I won't point fingers and say it's his or her fault that I'm not where I want to be, but I will say that the ignorance of others has ruined many lives.

Commentary

When I read George's Potential, I cannot help but experience two separate, yet simultaneous, reactions. The first is one of deep sympathy, something which comes from a place of understanding that writing like this cannot come without a great deal of pain and personal experience. The second is anger, again coming from a place of deep understanding; however, this second reaction is much more broad. When I read this I am angry, not on behalf of the author, myself, or any of the numerous people I can think of who have failed in some way to live up to their potential due to a lack of support and being told, in combination, that they must try harder and that what they want is impossible, but because this sort of thing happens at all.

Great visionaries all seem to have one thing in common which is very visible and, I suspect, one thing in common which is much less apparent. The first thing they all have in common is that they advocate that nothing is impossible. Do what you love, do it until you are good at it, and never listen to the people who will say you can't do it. This is the message of the greatest individuals in our history. In fact, this message is the proof of their brilliance, proof that they faced this sort of hardship and continued on. The second thing, the thing which I think has made their greatness possible, is a support system. People who, even if they thought the individual was crazy, refused to stand in the way, refused to gainsay or hinder, and who were willing to help their friend through the darkness which strikes at anyone who steps out of the mold.

George specifically tells us that "Everyone has a disability of some kind" (Potential), which strikes a personal chord with me, trying to come to terms with my mental diagnosis, but I think is more important than a personal anecdote would credit. Instead, think in terms of the handicaps we are all faced with, to one degree or another. Friends and family can launch you forward, or tie you down. Learning is unique to the individual, and yet education is standardized in such a way that only the average, of the correct learning style, with proper support, can succeed within the system. Society has a long list of unspoken laws which define who you are are allowed to be long before you have the opportunity to form a concept of who you are. These are things we all cope with, some more and some less, 'disabilities' we have in billions of variations.

The question is, with all this raw potential, is there any way we can overcome the systemic hindrances our culture insists upon?

- Rhiannin

War in the Schoolyard: A Continuation and Commentary

Rhiannin

Clarification, Additions, and Commentary on War in the School Yard

"Sticks and Stones may Break my Bones but Words Can Never Hurt Me."

Weren't you amazed the first time you said those words, your voice a proud sing-song as you declared the phrase you had been assured conveyed absolute invulnerability? A few seconds of absolute glowing confidence just before the phrase inevitably fails.

Two years ago I wrote *War in the School Yard* as a school assignment. Tasked with writing a memoir, I was initially daunted with the knowledge that there was nothing about me which was particularly note worthy. Certainly, I could come up with nothing that was worth the time and dedication required to write it down. Reading that essay now, it is hard not to compare what I wrote, and the great care with which I wrote it, to the raw memories I still have of its subject.

War in the School Yard is concerned with the period between my enrollment in preschool and the end of fourth grade, with only the tiniest mention of the rest of my life to that point. Amy and Michelle are both memories from kindergarten through second grade. Contained within a single paragraph, four of its five sentences, is a single additional event occurring in fourth grade. Looking at it now, with perhaps a bit more distance from the pain of those memories, I feel I should fill in a few more of the blanks.

War in the School Yard glosses over several things. For one, I was being physically harmed by the end of kindergarten. This did not stop the entire time I attended that elementary school. Indeed as I got older I was eventually forced to learn to defend myself against attacks, individual and group. I have at least one memory of being held down as other children proceeded to beat me. For those who would say that my case is extreme, I can neither confirm nor deny that opinion. In my experience people who were and are bullied are like me in that they also tend to make light of their experiences, speaking of them honestly in only the rarest moments with only the most trusted of friends.

For the rest going into detail would take too long, which was some of the motivation behind excluding my experiences in Colorado from the original essay. For the rest of my motivation I can say only that at the time including my experiences was both too difficult and too risky.

I will say, now, that the cycle of bullying progressed from physical to verbal and mental. From there isolation was an obvious result and reaction, and my isolation led to further rumors, and eventually sexual abuse by my peers. By middle school I actually had to enroll in a day program at Children's Hospital for treatment because I had a condition called School Refusal. I was afraid, to the point of panic attacks, of attending my middle school, of being near my middle school, of seeing it, speaking about it.

Even after I returned to middle school, eventually escaping into high school, my tour of duty in the school yard war was not complete. Rumors are told about everyone in high school, or so I am led to believe. So at the time I did my best to ignore those. When my friends and I were made fun of for showing emotion (often because of difficulties unrelated to school itself) others mocking us openly (in one instance as a group of us tried to comfort a crying friend a group of jocks gathered nearby, the one in the center pretending to cry as the rest crowded around and 'comforted' loudly), we ignored them, so they started to throw snowballs at us. The few that connected were mostly ice and left bruises. Situations turned mildly physical, and in a few instances I was directly threatened. The one time I reported such a threat, with another witness to back me up, my report was largely ignored and the person who threatened me was called into the office but otherwise received no punishment.

Between the actual bullying and the adult response, which was universally non-existent or harmful in it's own right, I grew up thinking not only that there was nothing else, that this was always what it would be like for me, but also that I deserved it and that for one reason or another I was defective. My defensive mechanism, like many others who suffer from bullying, was actually to internalize the issue, legitimizing my tormentors and rapidly accelerating the decline of my own self-esteem. By the time I was in high school my self-esteem can be best described as self-loathing, further complicating every interaction, even perfectly innocent ones.

As a conclusion to this time-line I spent two weeks in a psychiatric ward my freshman year of college. It didn't take more than a couple days before I was told that PTSD was a real possibility. PTSD was included in my diagnosis on my release papers.

I don't want my story to end here. War in the School Yard is a part of the story, the introduction to several chapters of my personal life story. Those are chapters I cannot erase no matter how much I may want to. But my story doesn't end there.

More important than anything else in the fight against bullying, my story isn't over! The story isn't over. The war hasn't been won by either side until the pen stops moving. Every suicide is a victory for the culture of bullying, and every survivor is a victory for the fight to end it!

Why do I say the culture of bullying rather than the bullies? Two reasons, for one thing, no one is fighting so that children have the right to torment other children the way I was tormented. Also, bullying is self-perpetuating, and it is the culture that has to change before bullying does. Despite no tolerance policies, bullying is often an invisible plague of our school system. Schools like my elementary in Chicago come with a policy of "Don't Ask, Don't Tell" when it comes to the social war. Teachers don't ask if the bullied are bullied, and even if they do, the students are bound by an internal code to deny what's happening. Interventions, when they come, need to be skillfully negotiated, with careful attention paid to every child involved, the victims and the perpetrators both. We can't fight bullying until we understand it. That means understanding the motivations, the repercussions, how it gets perpetuated, and how it happens. Until we understand all of those things bullying will continue under the eyes of even the most watchful instructors.

As I've grown up I've realized something that, had you told my eight-year-old self she would have said you were lying. Adults are bullies too.

The crux of changing our school yards is more than changing and policing the behavior of our children. We are tasked with changing and policing our *own* behavior. As a child, and then as a teenager, I have been bullied by children and I have been bullied by *adults*. There were some authority figures in my life who, through either negligence, prejudice, or malice, bullied me. If you want examples of adult bullies you need look no farther than many of our CEO's, our Politicians, and yes, our Administrators, our Teachers.

Bullying is an epidemic. We live the lives of the bullied and the bullies. We pass the tradition down to our children, just as we pass down the abuse from above to below. To change the culture of bullying we must examine our culture. To change the culture of bullying we must start at both ends, we must change the cultures of our children, and we much change the cultures in which we indulge ourselves.

I have survived to tell my story. Not all do. Even now people are succumbing to this war, some while still on the battlefield in the middle of their fight, some succumbing to their wounds, and still others will live on, drained mutilated and broken. Some will escape, bearing scars, bleeding, tired, and scared, but alive.

Mirrored

Cheyenne

He just needed to be seen.
Like a lost cause, you could see him stumbling in the
line opposite of his dreams,
told that kids will be kids, but nobody seemed to know
that the bruises on his arms
were the shape of his broken heart.
I guess he could only go so far
with chains the shape of fingerprints around his wrists,
the silent judgment of fellow playground kids stopped
him from fighting back.
He got used to getting the wind knocked out of him like
the time he got his teeth knocked out with a bat,
but the thing that made him cry at night wasn't the fact
that his chest showed a black and blue war that was
being fought,
but the fact that his reflection in the mirror
hated him, too.

Commentary

Mirror, mirror on the wall, who is the most tortured of all? This piece. written by Cheyenne, really expresses this kind of bullying in a new light. Most of the time when I hear or read about this kind of bullying it is painfully ignorant and very unappealing. The thing that I really think stands out about this piece is that it has incredibly visual metaphors that really express what the feeling is like. You can almost feel the chains weighing on you as you read further. The most fascinating part for me, though, is that it is written as if the boy is in elementary school but is even more of a reality when applied to a middle or high school setting.

- George

One of the things I love about this piece – and one of the things which makes it such a good ending to this section – is that it focuses on the psychological effects of bullying. This poem reminds us that a look, a word, or an attitude can do just as much damage as slamming someone up against a wall. Why? Because the worst damage is the damage done inside. And when it gets to the point where the Bullied believe the lies others have told them, they begin to bully themselves. External abusers aren't needed, because the Bullied are already trapped inside the cage of abuse and lies. This psychological effect may be better known than some of the details about bullying portrayed in this chapter, but that doesn't make it any less crucial – or deadly.

- Megan

Response to Bullying

David Romig

This chapter on bullying strikes me to the core of my being. It reminds me that part of the reason I entered into the helping professions, in the schools, was due to my own experiences with bullying as a child. In first grade, I spent significant time in the office for fighting against my tormentors. Subsequently, the bullies learned only to attack me in groups, in which two or three kids would hold me, while one or two more would hit me in the stomach so that no bruises could be seen. It was only my word against all of them. What I learned from this experience was that the bullies in our society are the winners, the jocks, whom we celebrate. Those of us who fight back against the system will be punished by those in power, the adults. I remember dreaming as a child about wanting to blow up the school with all the bullies in it, but I knew better than to ever express my wishes to anyone other than my closest friends. And, knowing how I was brought up, I also knew I would never act on such feelings.

As an adult, I wanted to make a difference and help those kids like me, who were the victims. What I have learned in our schools is that over the years with "No Tolerance" policies the bullies have become much more subtle. I see far less blatant physical aggression. After reading these young authors' stories, I realize that the things said and done now are every bit as hurtful, if not more so.

I also find the system and our culture continues to fail the victims of bullying. When I have asked students to share their stories of being a victim with school administrators, we are told that the administration must follow due process, which means, in reality the bully will be called in to talk with an administrator. The bully then will deny the allegations, and because, it is just a case of he said he did, the administrators hands are tied and they cannot do anything. Again, this allows the bullies to win. My students no longer wish to share with me when they are victimized; they feel there is no point telling when nothing will be done to help them. I further feel that not unlike the students, those with the power (administrators) often perpetuate the problems and often themselves are bullies, at times, undermining my efforts to support the victims. After reading these stories, and knowing my own current experiences in the schools, it leaves me feeling that nothing has changed or improved for victims of bullying. In fact, things may actually be worse. These days, victims are turning more frequently to violence against their tormentors and toward themselves. As a result, I am left feeling all the more helpless and hopeless to change what is going on. When will we really listen to what is happening to our youth? Perhaps, if we really listen, maybe we, as a society, will be more willing to stand-up and agree that we must change the system, meaning our culture and our responses to both bullies and victims, maybe then positive change will be possible.

Summary

Eric Smith

Memories of being the victim and of being the perpetrator of bullying; things and feelings long forgotten are brought to the surface as I read this chapter. Perhaps that is the problem with society's response to bullying. We don't really remember it. It was too painful so we buried the memories and thus the reality. Or, our lives became so complicated over time that there was no room in our active consciousness for recalling the realities we faced in our youth. And maybe we don't want to acknowledge the reality of bullying – that it is as common in adulthood as it is in youth.

Consider what Rhiannin reveals about the "war" that pits even preschoolers against each other. Our young at that age are really a reflection of their parents. They have not grown enough to make conscious choices to be individuals apart from families and similar social groups. So they reflect attitudes that adults they are most familiar with demonstrate. Oh, those adults probably don't mean to perpetuate stereotypes and attitudes of exclusion, but they are there none-the-less. And those attitudes carry over to our children, whether or not we intend that result.

But Rhiannin points out more in her exposition. Our children quickly develop a code of silence. Whether it is due to the response of both adults (which never seems to help) and the bullies (who increase the pressure when caught) is not clear.

One of the larger problems in dealing with bullying when it is "witnessed" is that often we see only the response to being bullied and discipline the responder, again victimizing her or him. Once the overt behavior has been corrected or disciplined, we assume we have handled the situation. But, as Rhiannin points out, we missed the actual instigators and we have set up a scenario where victims are less likely to report because they will be further victimized. We create a culture that not only is oblivious to what is going on, but actually perpetuates it.

George gives us another view when he discusses the potential we all have. It can be nurtured or it can be diminished by those around us, especially when we are young. And diminishing can be unintentional. In "Potential," George shows us that well-meaning adults, in a position to support our young people, may end up doing the opposite, even becoming the bullies we are trying to prevent. It can be as simple as telling a person to "work harder" over and over without helping them find concrete ways to succeed. It becomes the mantra of the teacher or counselor. And, it becomes bullying to the youth constantly receiving the mantra but no actual assistance. The adults in a position to help have become part of the problem – bullies diminishing the potential of the students they are trying to help. When we rely on "standard" responses in order to be efficient in our jobs and dealing with large numbers of people, we overlook the fact that each individual is different and needs to be treated as an individual. Certainly the systems works for many, but they do not work for all. And for those who don't "fit" the system becomes a bully.

Rhiannin takes this discussion further in her commentary on the "War in the Schoolyard." It is intensely personal and it points out how bullying progresses for the victim from simple words to violence. And, the adult response is often non-existent or makes things worse because the adults don't get to the root causes and often miss the perpetrators, seeing only the responders. So our young hide the facts from the adults they no longer trust. Some don't survive, succumbing to the negativity. Those who do survive are often damaged in some way. Think back through your memories - are you sure you weren't damaged?

Perhaps that is the worst impact of bullying - we do become damaged, both the victim and the bully. Consider what Cheyenne tells us - eventually the victim (and probably the bully) begins to believe what is said and done. Then they become the worst sort of bully - they bully themselves, continuing the spiral, even in the absence of external bullies.

So, what can we do? Rhiannin reminds us that bullying is a cultural thing, perpetuated by the bullies and the victims as they mature and become the carriers of society. Thus all of our so-called anti-bullying programs are doomed to failure unless we address the culture. We have to convince everyone, adults and youth alike, to break the cycle. It starts with realizing that most bullies are victims, too. It may be a situation at home or in the school. It may be as simple as a label applied without thinking to a young person that starts it.

We must come together with a common purpose in supporting each other in reaching her or his individual potential. And, when things arise, as they always will, we must work with both the victim and the perpetrator to find solutions and repair damage. Finally, we must agree that the cycle must be broken in favor of a more positive one. Let us learn from our youth, both their mistakes and their solutions.

Broken Schools

"The educational system is broken!"

It is a common headline. It seems to slap us in the face week in and week out. But what do we do about it? We hear that test scores in the US are really bad and getting worse when compared to other countries. But how do we improve them? We have ten years of this program or that program, yet we don't see progress. We listen to the pundits - the so-called experts. They say they know what is wrong, but they contradict each other. And often they are not teachers or people who actually work with our young people.

We look at test scores and if they don't improve, we jump to the conclusion that our teachers are bad. But, do we look at the tests? They are often biased one way or another. They test for facts, not creativity. They measure a core of knowledge or basic skills, but not thinking. Worse, they assume that all students are the same. But they aren't.

What if we asked a different question, asked a different group? Schools all over the country are essentially the same, cut from our industrial age past. Oh, we have exceptions. But they are few and far between. So, who should we ask and what should we ask them? Why not try asking the students themselves? What might they be able to tell us...

- Eric Smith

School

George

We're sorry to tell you that's not the answer
You are correct but what we seek is perfection.
It might help if you were a soldier,
Then we could make you stand at attention.
But the eyes have it, you'll be the dancer.
And when we're done, you'll be lost in detention.
But, don't fret, for ignorance is the answer
To solve your little dedication
For we will break you forever
Till the desired answer is the only thing left in the wake
of devastation.

Education

Rhiannin

In preschool the thought of learning is exciting
We would sit in play houses
And pretend that we knew everything
We'd open books we couldn't read
And spout truths we didn't comprehend

By third grade you're left wondering.
When does the fun begin?

I remember the feeling

Being taped to my textbooks
And the question was never
What would you like to learn,
It was always,
What can we pigeon-hole teach you?
How many words can we shove down your throat
to be regurgitated later
How thoroughly can we train you
to answer questions on demand

Reading was a dream
A goal they took away from me
Because what my progress reports measured
Was never my ability to think and choose for myself.

And though it was my choice to read
No standard test could ask me
From whence came my love of story
When did immeasurable begin to mean unimportant
Unneeded
Unnecessary
Under-appreciated and inconsequential?

There are so many things about me

that cannot be written on paper,
Yet they chain me to these under-mining definitions
They look at two dimensional descriptions and think
that they see the
real me?

Who decided that it was more important to learn about
Europe
Than Africa and China
Who considered that History should really be
A modified age-appropriate reality
And that the most important bits
Ought to be glossed over for so long
That when the true versions are finally told
It's easy to understand not believing?

So Glad

Megan

Reaction to Rhiannin's "Education"

Oh. My. Word. This is still one of the most powerful pieces for me, because it puts in smooth, clear lines what my mom always tried to tell me about why my brother and I were home-schooled. I heard phrases like "they don't teach kids how to learn or think, they teach you how to take a test", uttered in my mother's tone of pent-up frustration. I saw with my own eyes the way the kids on our street approached their schoolwork. They came at it with an air of boredom, veiled disgust, and complete disinterest, even when faced with something cool, like the flipping of the earth's magnetic field. My brother and I came at subjects or new information with shining eyes, ready and eager to learn. Even if it was something boring like math, we approached it with a resigned dislike, but not with the boredom and desolate frustration of our public schooled friends. They looked as though they were even tired of being frustrated with their schoolwork. Yet somehow, all those stories about the inadequacy of public school and even the attitudes of the neighbor kids were never quite real until I read this poem.

This poem gave me confirmation of what I'd always heard, but never completely believed: that you don't "learn" in public school, you're taught how to take a test. That the social pressures and bullying that go on in public school can leave you scarred for the rest of your life. That the subject matter is so boring and stupid that any kid with half a brain gives up half-way through, or else they struggle, because the format being taught is opposite the way their brain works, so they can hardly understand any of it.

I am so glad I was home-schooled, and brought up on Nova and Bill Nye, Mr. Rogers and The Magic School Bus; that I spent afternoons down at the creek, hunting fossils with Mom, or listening to songs on the characteristics of mammals, so that I astounded the teachers of the nature programs to which my mother took me. I am so grateful that I never had to feel pressured because of my body; that my worst social troubles were spending Middle School without any "public-schooled" friends, because their culture was made up of things I'd never heard of. I am so glad I grew up surrounded by friends I could count on and cling to and hang out with. Reading this poem made me realize just how blessed and lucky I am to have been home-schooled.

Focus

Megan

"Focus," I mutter to myself as I bend over my math test. Focus is such an interesting word. It gets said a lot at our house, since we all have ADD. Heh, you can spot a half-trained (or all-trained) ADD'er anywhere by the way they mutter "focus" to themselves at odd intervals, especially when accompanied by clicking a pen. It's an interesting thing, but the speed of the pen clicking directly correlates to how often they mutter "focus", and has an inverse relationship to how interesting the subject at hand is. The more boring something is, the faster the pen goes and the more often they mutter "focus" to themselves-

"Focus!" I set my pen down on the page.

What is the domain if Y=sinX? Domain. I've had this before. It has something to do with X…the value of X, perhaps? Yes, that's it. But how do I figure it out? I glance around my room, as if hoping something will jar my memory. There's a bird perched on the tree outside my window. Not a robin. It's another one of those mostly tan ones. Mom would know, but-

"Focus!"

My Latin final is next Tuesday. "Focus" might be on the vocabulary. Such an interesting word, 'focus'. In English, it means the point at which something is, well, focused. What it's aimed towards. Or it can be a verb, as in "to focus", or the imperative –

"FOCUS!" I bend back over my paper. Domain of Y=sinX. I punch a few numbers into my calculator. I glance at the possible answers. I don't remember how to do this. And the longer I stay on the problem the more distracted I'll get. I circle "all real numbers" and move onto the next question: What is the range of Y=sinX? Phooey. Range was Y, but...I glance up and my eye alights on my Latin poster, jogging my previous thought.

The coolest thing about "focus" is that in Latin it means "hearth, home, family, (household gods)" or something of that sort. I have it written down somewhere.

"Focus!"

It's such a neat thought, that one's "focus" is one's home or family, isn't it? What was it the Bible said about that? "The eye is the lamp of the body..." In the margin I had written "focus?". No idea if that's right or not, but I felt there was something to it. More like "where your treasure is, there will your heart be also", perhaps. If your focus is on something good, like home and family, you're more likely to be a cheerful, happy person –

"FOCUS!" says a voice that isn't mine.

I jerk in my chair and try to spin round, and succeed in nearly falling over. My chair clatters to the floor.

Dad is standing in my doorway, grinning. "How's that math test going, Meg?"

"I'm working on it," I mutter, righting my chair.

"Are you *focusing*?"

I glare at him. "I am now."

I turn back to my math test. *Focus.*

So Let Me Go Already

Cheyenne

I'm at conflict with myself.
I grew up knowing what I want, and what others expect of me,
but sometimes I'm not sure that if what I want to be is what I should be.
How can you expect me to get straight A's when every time I look at the board,
Instead of seeing the answer I only see a reflection of my frown?
I'm asked the question "Are you planning on graduating?" with my answer already chosen.
And for a while I thought their answer was the same as my own,
but lately I'm not so sure.
I want to be a teacher - but how can I even think about stepping in front of the same board
that has held no interest for me since the last time I was told I was failing?
I don't know what to do anymore.
Every time I mess up the image of me and my older sister blend a little more together.
I don't want to be considered a bad influence on my friends and my little sisters.

I'm left sitting here feeling like my efforts aren't hard enough, when I've stuck my neck out for an A one too many times.
To bad to get the grade you have to be okay with the noose letting you hang when it said it would make you fly.
So I stop putting the effort into my schooling and start putting effort into what I want for once.
Why is that so wrong?
My GPA should not define my life.
You should not be able to assume which side of the world I sleep on by my test grades.
School does nothing but stress me out, so why is it so bad to cast it aside?
I'm open to education but not this shit system that puts my learning in someones else's hands.
My grade point average isn't because I'm lazy.
It's because when I walk into the class, I'm already preparing myself for this lecture,
This feeling of disappointment that they'll give when I tell the teacher that I didn't do my homework again.
This "look" like my future is dim -
and that they might as well give up on me already because
there are other millions of children that have more of a chance of turning out better than I could ever have dreamed of becoming.
So let me go already,

Class A fuck up but barely class D when it comes to
everything else.
Maybe I should take the teachers advice and just drop
out.
But, they don't say it that way, pursuing your GED is how
it comes out.
But ask anyone in my family who was told the exact
same thing,
they'll tell you a different story.
One where they worked minimum wage and can barely
support a family in this day and age,
and how I'm the only chance to make my parents proud.

I'm so sorry, but if this is how life is, I want a way out.
So let me go already.

Commentary

School is an interesting proposition for anyone who doesn't fit into the conventional mold. There are too many people who are like this specifically, wanting to be teachers but uncertain how to do that when they actually hate what school looks like today. People who don't fit society often seem to want to be teachers, or to assume other positions of authority and trust, wanting to help other people like themselves navigate the complicated waters of a society which values standardization in all things, including people. Unfortunately this desire is in direct opposition with the things required to be successful in today's middle class worker production factories (schools).

Standardized testing, standardized curriculum, and standardized teaching methods are all becoming stricter, the goal being to have as uniform an education as possible which conforms to the needs of the largest number of children, while accommodating the lowest common denominator. Basically the curriculum needs to be similar enough that a large number of teachers should be able to execute it within the range of difference permitted by the test upon which the student, school, and teacher are all judged. It also needs to be simple enough that the dullest, least motivated student in any given class has at least a chance of succeeding with the material. At the same time parental pressure, and societal pressure in general, is on students and teachers both to produce A students with 4.0 GPA's even though the grading system is based on the average student, putting in an average amount of work, receiving a C. 4.0 students are not supposed to make up more than 10% of the population of a school, and yet the system is producing a larger number of 4.0's by simplifying the classes and lowering the requirements.

All of this combines to make someone who wants more out of their education than rote memorization of facts, and impersonal lessons which may or may not prove to have any relevance in life, incredibly bored and likely to disengage. School has become both too important in life, and undervalued. Students, parents, and the officials designing our school system all currently take for granted that students will be graduating with extraordinary GPA's and paper qualifications because that is the expectation. It has become secondary to actually encourage superiority, difference, or those who are at the top of the range of intelligence.

The fact of the matter is that our schools are stifling creativity and individuality, not to mention those who are simply more intellectually advanced than the curriculum they are presented with, destroying their self-confidence, telling them they are problem children until it becomes true, and squashing the hopes of the different to make a difference.

Cheyenne's piece to me effectively highlights these problems, and the frustration, from the perspective of someone who was being held back and hurt by the system whose job it was to encourage and help her.

- Rhiannin

Summary

David Benke

How do we do it? How do we take children who are excited about learning and turn them into school haters? Rhiannin reminds us that "In preschool the thought of learning is exciting." Consider a scene in "Monty Python's The Meaning of Life" where John Cleese succeeds in making a live demonstration of sex boring for a group of adolescent boys; a highly appropriate parody of school. It shows that the right kind of educator, or educational environment, can suck the fun out of anything. Megan says it best, "I saw with my own eyes the way the kids on our street approached their schoolwork. They came at it with an air of boredom, veiled disgust, and complete un- interest, even when faced with something cool, like the flipping of the earth's magnetic field." What is the problem? What causes children to sit in school everyday and think, "Well Teach, what are you going to make me learn today?" I think that it is the lack of play. For millennia humans learned by play and story telling and both have been rooted out of education with increasing fervor in the past ten years because play isn't an efficient way to study for a standardized test. Play educates in a way that is fun, informs while conveying coolness, and more importantly builds a complete person but in our modern educational paradigm those things aren't testable and therefore they are not valuable.

During the industrial revolution factory solutions were applied to education to make people into standardized parts suitable to be plugged into the manufacturing process. Now we are supposedly in a post industrial age but the effort to make children fit into predetermined slots is greater than ever. The writings in this chapter lament the pressure of modern education but not the pressure to think or perform. Mainly they lament the pressure to be the same and perform in a predetermined way. Predetermined and predictable has become what school is, which is why George simply entitled his piece "School." Some students play the game and look for the bright spots of caring, interested teachers that, unfortunately, grow ever fainter, but some, like Cheyenne in "So Let Me Go Already," refuse to let their GPA define their life.

It is that pressure for the same answer that hurts kids and that should be enough to make us question educational practice, but it also hurts our society. We hear the cry, "The United States needs more engineers." But, don't we really need more creative engineering solutions? Don't we need different answers instead of more of the same answer? Ironically, and unfortunately, in a time desperate for more creative thinking, there is a concentrated drive to reward standardized performance. When society needs different answers, school is encouraging the same answer on the same test delivered at the same time from everyone; just make sure to show your work. When we need to celebrate Megan's brilliantly creative divergence, instead we reward "Focus." Oh we claim to be diverse, but it is diverse superficiality not diversity of thought. School should be gumbo with andouille sausage, chicken thighs, cajun trinity, filé, and Virginia ham. Instead it is cream of wheat. No wonder our youth want to spew it out of their mouths.

What Makes Us Who We Are, Or Might Be

Is it "nature" or "nurture?" Or is it some divine intercession? This argument about what makes people the beings they are has been going on probably as long as people have considered beginnings and endings philosophically. It can be an interesting discussion, at least when kept to the abstract.

But as we bring the argument closer and closer to ourselves, does it clarify things? Or raise a fog of confusion? It is too simplistic to say one or the other. Certainly there is an impact of genetics on our physical selves. And there may be a genetic component to our tendency toward various psychological conditions. But, the world around us, with the impact of chemicals and environment, can also alter our physical and psychological realities, influencing our behavior and thinking. So, which is it? nature or nurture?

Being exposed to different philosophies and lifestyles influences how we choose to live; so too, can our biology and even accident and injury. And that may be the key. When we look at ourselves, the question really is not nature, nurture, or divinity. Instead it is choosing which will influence us when. Sometimes it is conscious choice, sometimes we don't think about it. Indeed, as we get older, I suspect we think less and less, coasting along on the sum of earlier influence and becoming "set in our ways." What would happen if we made a conscious effort be like we were in our youth - asking questions and seeking our own paths? Might we find that the world has been changing and follow? Might we find it in our hearts to be more forgiving and accepting? Might we celebrate a renewed youth and joy in seeing a new world?

What does make us who we are or, more importantly, who we might become?

- Eric Smith

Humanity

George

I would rather die! Yelled the poor young man as he was tattooed with his number. He no longer had a name. He was known by his number. He didn't even get to choose his number. Then he was placed into a cage. He was given a cage and treated like an animal. He wasn't worthy of walls or a ceiling or running water. The only human aspect left to him was his appearance. When he looked at the others in the cages around him they looked at him with disappointed glances. He couldn't even find comfort in the fact that he wasn't alone. His life was reduced to waiting, praying for lightning to strike him.

> "He just said: "Don't have no money." The owner yelled: "Why in hell did you come in here and eat my food if you don't have no money? That food cost me money." Mister Williams jumped over the counter and knocked the wino off his stool and beat him over the head with a pop bottle. Then he stepped back and watched the wino bleed. Then he kicked him. And he kicked him again."(Gregory D)

In this situation, the man in front of the counter without money wasn't worth anything. He was measured by his money not by the man he was. When the owner of the store found out he'd eaten without any money, he decided that the man wasn't worth the time to get out of his store. Instead he thought the man would pay for his food by enduring a beating.

What is dehumanization? It is the struggle of one human being trying to convince himself that he is of a greater state than that of another human.

> "At the core of evil is the process of dehumanization by which certain other people or collectives of them, are depicted as less than human, as non comparable in humanity or personal dignity to those who do the labeling. Prejudice employs negative stereotypes in images or verbally abusive terms to demean and degrade the objects of its narrow view of superiority over these allegedly inferior persons." (Zimbardo P)

It is what the Nazi's did to make gassing the Jews seem "not so bad." When you dehumanize a person you haven't taken away any part of their humanity; you've only demented your own perspective of that person's humanity to accommodate your own lacking of strength to know the difference. When you dehumanize someone, you have not altered them in anyway. The act of dehumanization is more dehumanizing to the person inflicting it than the recipient. In a pathetic attempt to rationalize their evil deed some will try and dehumanize another. To their dismay, they will have no real effect on the humanity of anyone else.

Humanity can't be measured. It can't be taken away. It can't be reduced. It can only be the tool of a great evil to justify the perpetrator's horrible actions. We all have humanity, and an equal amount, at that. Humanity is the idea that we have value in just existing. It is not given to us, therefore it can not be taken away. Any person that believes he is capable of dehumanizing another has already dehumanized himself and nothing more.

Dreams

Rhiannin

Living dreams in which I scream insanity,
Waking cry bloodied tears
For the living reality
In which this world can never know,
The glory of
A dreaming conception
Come true

Living dreams
Are but nightmares seen
Through the lens
Of our false reality

Why when I dream
Must I wake again to see
The bitter corruption that eats away
The honest glory
Of the reality
Of nightly drifting

Bloodied faces darkened
In the light of the nightmares they alone have seen.
For this mutually dissimilar mirror of perception
Through which a rose half-wilted is
Beautiful trash,

Is the lens through which we perceive
Contingent on the flavor of our dreams?
And the innocent light through which, it seems, most
see
this world lost in part to catastrophe,
Merely the result of
Bighearted dreams,
To similar to the cruelties surrounding those both blind
and free
To cast lights of virtue
And shadows of sin across perception?

For in all my darkness,
In my dreams I see impossible perfections,
And I cannot help but bleed in tears
For all those fantasies which
Waking
Will never be seen.

Influence

Brittney

Influence is not a matter of the conscious mind.
The words that you hear
Keep you confined.
When staring in a mirror
Flaws are all too easy to find
Insecurities are hard to cure
Attitude acts as a lure
To this you have always been blind
You never learned how to steer
And though you search you don't find
For they taught you how to fear
And on your fear they dine.
They use it to keep you in line.
Memories you once held dear
They get lost in time.
It's influence that binds you.
The world around you defines you.

In Pictures

Rhiannin

She had wondered at the pictures. Having met him she knew the vulnerability. It was in his eyes, his mouth, and she knew people. It had been in the way he kissed her, the touch of his hands that was afraid for more than her sake alone, even as they were greedy for more. But most of all it had been in the pictures. Some of them, the younger ones, showed pain and strength combined, a face that had seen more than it should, but not more than it could take. It was a face beyond its years, but still young, trusting. The man he had become was not, though he made a good show of it. Hesitance masked so easily by recklessness, for eyes not used to seeing past such lies. Lies told even to the teller himself. Not all the time, for he was stronger than that, but when he needed them. Because he was not stronger than the truth. His truth, his lies. The pictures showed the change. Young versions of the man hurt but whole, healing from past ills, eager for a future he was certain of. And she had wondered at that, because the man he had become was certain of nothing, trusting of no one. His heart was his own, closely guarded, locked as far away as he dared keep it. His secrets bared only in those rare moments of weakness that combined with those few that he thought he might possibly be able to trust. This was not the man foretold in those pictures, not the early ones. This was a man shadowed by half-healed ills and fresh bleeding wounds that left him no haven to tend to either problem.

A truncated version of his past led her to think she might have the answer, a stay in juvie. It's not hard to imagine, not after the life she's lived, the way she's shared the brains and memories of others. She can imagine him, scared, but somewhat confident at first, not too worried about what surely must have been an exaggerated lie on the part of the adults in his life. It's easy to imagine the way he grew at first more afraid, and then less. She pictures fights, the boy learning more about fighting from these other boys that also saw too much, knew too much, did too much for their young age. She can picture alliances, and hatreds, and the fear of starting over when moved. It's not that she knows any of these things, not as he knows them, but she can see them in the image trapped behind a glass screen. And she knows them as she knows him, the surface, and horns of something deeper, things that created the man, but not the thoughts that man hides.

Not because she couldn't see those if she wanted to, if he let her, but because he hides them from himself and she must respect those barriers. Failure to do so risks too much of them both, and her heart and brain combine in agreement to warn her of the grave vulnerability offered by such a path.

Yet, this is not the truth she was looking for. These horrors, and the wounds left by them, were merely the healing wounds. These he is more than strong enough to overcome, given the time. He's strong this one, more than he gives himself credit for, more than many give him credit for now, because he has to hide both the strength and the weakness. And people think him the weaker for it, they see him and they see the faults he himself now sees. Hard to heal from wounds when people keep poking the bruises, pouring vinegar over the cuts, tearing off scabs just as they heal. Because the real wound is much deeper than anything mere children and their jailers could cause. The pictures she's seen show the truth of that, because that face is the face of someone that saw those things, experienced them and more, and survived. Hardened some, this is true, anyone would be, but still allowing the most important vulnerabilities to exist. In those pictures, those vulnerabilities are exactly what he needs, not the masks he needs now. Yet for the man she knows now, those vulnerabilities are torn open, and he hides them.

Maybe she has the answer for why his pictures changed. He was healing, this is true. He'd found her, not the girl that sees his pictures and wonders at the change, but the girl that made them change. The other one. She's not unusually cruel, it is not something she did a'purpose, but the act is there. The question of why... It can't be answered. Though, the watcher can imagine that too. She can picture the two of them, innocent and shy at first, anxious nerves of all teens cast in romantic light. It isn't hard to picture the process, nervous at first and then on to comfortable amore. Past that, the image is almost entirely of her crafting, though again his eyes tell much of the truth. The glow of her, the other girl, never left his eyes, but as time wore on, love faded on one side. There are pictures of them too, pictures that she that watches had seen, though she'd never seen the reality. Always she searched for the answers in him, the one she knew, not in her, the other, the one she did not. But there was the answer, for when he was smiling contentedly, happily letting himself be carried along, healed a little more every day by present optimism, the other was questioning that future they'd laid. She said yes, presented with a ring, and he planned, happily, excitedly, but most importantly, contentedly, while the other girl questioned. And while she questioned, he did not see. So when she left... There was no reserve.

He had given all, for when thinking of futures, all or nothing is a good way to plan. He had given all, and she would give now nothing.

And the future he had laid crumbled. The wounds that had been healing nearly burst, nearly joined newly forged companions. Together they nearly bled him out of forever. But he pulled himself back from that brink. Even away from the brink, though the healing had ended. He bandaged himself carefully, half hoping he'd fail, that the blood would keep pounding out through the gashes. It didn't. Some days instead of bandaging he ripped them open. Still he staggered on, gathering pieces and seeing if somehow he could reforge the whole he had been familiar with. In time he'd realize that whole was gone. In time he'd choose another girl, though he couldn't claim the same commitment to her. He couldn't find himself, couldn't figure out how to get back to the boy who wasn't afraid to be vulnerable with his love.

The girl watching the pictures sees it all now. The change, and the reasons behind it. She sees why there is so much pain in him, why he hides it. Above all she sees why he doesn't want her to help with this pain. Much of him is still afraid, afraid to let her in. Because although he is not the same, something about her makes him feel a way he hasn't in a long time. He doesn't know why. He certainly hasn't known her long enough, nor has she known him, and she knows this. The time isn't there, but perhaps a spark is, and that frightens him. Because he has wounds that haven't healed, and a mask he can't yet drop, and he can't use her to heal those things. He can't hurt her. She looks at the pictures and sees the pain she wants to help him heal, and she looks at him, the man she sees now. She wants to remind him that a knight in shinning armor has never proven himself in battle or in fire. She wants to show him that while the pieces don't fit together to create the boy that he was, and maybe they don't fit together to be the man he wanted to become, but that the glass and crystal of him shines no less brightly for the burns, the gashes, the blood, and most especially not for the tears. And while it is no longer the masterpiece it was once meant to be, it is still a masterpiece. This she can see outside the pictures. This isn't just in his eyes or his mouth, but his voice, his laugh, his hair, his clothes. Even his scent tells her this. But it is most in his gaze, a gaze that conveys everything, and nothing. His truth and his lies can not be captured in a picture as they can in his gaze. The pictures told her the story, once he'd let her in enough to see the truth, but the story only matters so far as it has taken the person. And he is a person, good enough as to make them that see his past wonder how this man of bright glass and crystal, of dark titanium and steel, of delicate silver and gold, and the greens of grass, the blues of sky, the reds of passion, the purples of power, to wonder how this man came forged shining from what was. And she wonders how to show him all she sees outside the pictures. She hopes that she can show him, so he can forgive himself the pain, so he can heal. Because for the Watcher the important thing is not the past but the future, and her only hope to show him the glory of his creation, so that he doesn't lose the future for which he was made. So he doesn't lose the future that was made for him.

The Will to Choose

Vlad

When I was a little kid, I didn't know what the world was like. I was in the orphanage; there family came first. Family to me was my friends. We all had the freedom to make our own life choices. This meant that we could do what we desired. I was a kid, I was not ready to make life decisions.

Sometimes I choose badly.

Some choices were easy to make and some were hard. Education was an easy choice to make - none of us wanted to go to school. Playing soccer and hanging out with friends was more important. Run or stand your ground. This decision was a hard one to make. When I had to make this decision I chose wrong. I was 12 years old and my Mom gave me one of the toughest choices of my life. She told me "I'm going to die soon, please come back for your birthday." I had no words to say, even my mind was silent.

Instead of coming back, I ran to my friends and away from the orphanage, making bad choices. A month and half passed and I still didn't see my Mom. I had been living with my friend for two weeks when I got a call. It was from the orphanage telling me that my Mom had died.

After my Moms death I was making even worse choices. I was putting myself to sleep with alcohol, I didn't care about school, and my own safety didn't concern me. Even now when I see people drink alcohol it brings back bad memories of what I did before Mom died. Those bad choices still haunt me today.

Before my Mom's death, I was given the chance to visit America. And I did. When I got to the United States, everything was different. The streets, places to eat, and people seemed more wealthy. A month passed really quickly and I had to return to my home. When I returned to the orphanage nothing had changed but my perspective. It was sad and depressing at the orphanage. I now knew what a real family was like. Before my Mom died, I was given a chance to come to America for a second time. But my poor life choices were causing the opportunity to come to America to slip away.

Sometimes I still choose badly.

But I didn't only make bad choices. I saved a young girl's life once. One day I was walking minding my own business when I saw my friend Liliana, the next thing I knew she fell through the ice. I instantly ran to save her. Within seconds I had her in my arms gasping for breath, walking toward the shore. When we got to the shore I set her down and gave her my jacket to warm her up. Once she caught her breath I walked her back to the orphanage.

Sometimes I choose well.

But the greatest and hardest decision I had to make was yet to be made. When I was 13 the second visit to America became a chance to be adopted and to stay in America for good, and I never looked back. Even though I'm in America, it is still just as easy to make bad choices. It's OK to make a bad choice as long as you don't make it twice. If I didn't have the free will, Liliana might have died that day in the lake, and I would still be in the orphanage dreaming about coming to America.

The Strength of Our Youth

Cheyenne

Young hands,
weak and frail,
hold so much.
Hold my heart
Hold my sanity
Hold my sin
Hold my innocence,
all the while holding,
gripping,
my finger
as you take your first steps
into a darkness that doesn't
seem so dark
in the light of you.

Summary

Eric

What does make us who we are? It is a difficult question when you try to reach specifics. Sure, we can speak generally about factors of personal history, family, even geography. But what is it really? Are there specific events or ideas? We all struggle with the question, when we have time for personal reflection. For your youth, the question is more immediate, perhaps because the cares of the world have not yet settled on their shoulders. Yet, as I read the chapter, I wonder whether it is true that the cares of the world are not yet known by them.

We begin with the concept of humanity and how all of us have been given humanity in equal measure. It cannot be taken from us, it is part of the definition of being human. Yet we are surrounded by people who try to dehumanize us in order to maintain the status quo or to make themselves feel superior. All you have to do is listen to the news for a little while. Immigration as an issue seems to fall into an "us over them" discussion – they are the outsiders and they are less than us. Conflicts in the middle east (or anywhere, really) devolve into "us versus them" and "we are better and we won't negotiate with those who are less than us." The cycle constantly repeats. In our cities, rival gangs act the same way. In countries facing revolution or race or ethnic conflict, it is the same. Yet, George reminds us that the attempt to dehumanize others really only destroys us. The process may seem to help build a group identity, but actually a group identity can only be built when everyone is treated with respect and the focus is on ideas.

And where do these ideas come from? Often they are the dreams and hopes of individuals, shared and grown into a movement. But, especially for our youth, dreams can be a challenge. Dreams of what might be always seem to fall before reality. It is a lament. But do those dreams really have to fall or fail? I suspect that our youth often see the world attacking their dreams and taking them away. It is what many people, not just our young, experience. But does it have to be that way? Enough strength and perseverance, along with support, can make the dreams come true. And the process of striving to reach those dreams goes a long way toward shaping who we become.

While our humanity cannot be taken, what we do with it can be shaped by forces outside ourselves. This influence can be for good or ill, depending on those around us and how they wield their influence. Unfortunately for our youth, such influence is often negative, sometimes with intent, often without, though the result may be the same. It seems that in our ever shrinking world the positive influences to shape us are increasingly difficult to find – too many possible influences competing for our attention.

Sometimes the things that influence who and what we are come from our willingness to be open and vulnerable. Our friendships and loves cannot be without vulnerability and risking ourselves. When they work out, we grow and thrive. But when they don't, we struggle. That struggle has, arguably, more impact on who we are or will become. We come away from broken relationships with scars, even though we may, in the end, find a way to move forward and risk again. It is a process and as Rhiannin reminds us, viewed from without, that process and our defenses are visible, even when we can't see them. Sometimes we give up and shut out the world. But if we have the strength, we can share and risk again. The picture is different, shaded by our experiences, but no less beautiful.

Still, it requires us to make the choice to risk again, to see the world and relationships as positive again.

Choice itself is an important aspect of the process of becoming. Vlad reminds us that we face choices on a daily basis and that sometimes we are not ready to make those choices. We have not been prepared well enough. And so, we make poor choices. The trick, though, is to recover when a poor choice is made, learn from it, and never make that mistake again. We learn from our choices and that knowledge, not the choices themselves, shapes us.

Yet, in the end, we find that our youth, especially, have a great deal of strength. They must to survive the complex situations and choices society requires they make. That strength also shapes them, indeed all of us. Being young today is more of a challenge than it was when I was young. The world is more complex, the pace faster, the choices more plentiful. When I was young, we chaffed under our perceived burdens. How much more do our youth wear under today's burdens?

Our youth do recognize that people are largely similar – all have the gift of humanity. But often and for selfish reasons, we choose to deny that humanity. They rightfully point out that denial only diminishes us and we should instead try to build each other. And we have great opportunities to support each other. Why should the dreams of the young become waking nightmares? We could change that, simply by listening and providing resources to chase positive dreams. In the process of helping our youth find positive dreams, we will also change the forces influencing them toward the positive. It is not true that words can't hurt us. When constantly inundated by them, if they are negative, we begin to believe. By the same token, if they are positive, we begin to believe and act in positive ways. Unfortunately, our youth often see only the negative. We have the power to change that perception, though it may be difficult.

In the end, these writers show us what we all know, but sometimes forget. The things that determine who we are or might be are complex – a mix of situation, people, attitudes, and choices. It is what and how we choose that ultimately determines what we become. May we all help each other make positive choices.

Friendship and Relationships

No man is an island, entire of itself, every man is a piece of the continent, a part of the main.

John Donne wrote these words in 1624 as part of Meditation 17, Devotions Upon Emergent Occasions. But we don't remember that part. Indeed most adults and youth alike don't know anything about John Donne. Still we remember the phrase or something like it.

No man is an island.

No person is an island.

No One is an island!

No matter how much we think we can do everything by ourselves, it isn't true. Human-kind is a social animal. While we do try to define ourselves on our own terms, that definition is determined, in part, by our relationships with others. The type and quality of our friendships reflect upon and to some extent define us, even to ourselves.

But relationships are tricky. We open up ourselves to one degree or another, risking hurt from relationship failures. When relationships work, we often take them for granted and let them coast along as steady states. When they don't work, we are hurt, confused, sometimes even give up. Is it worth the struggle to maintain when it hurts? As we get older, we often say no. And it is our loss. These struggles are common to us all. But when we are young, with less life experience and less time to become jaded, the levels of joy and pain can be heightened. May we read, relate, and remember that quality relationships, friendships, loves are worth fighting for and working to keep together.

- Eric Smith

How I Feel in 90 Words

Chad

You say that you hate to be objectified,
So why do you insist on lurking in the treasure trove?
You would have yourself conquered before you affirmed alliance.
You complain and complain but do nothing to change.
So burdened you have made yourself,
As to frighten off those who wish to help.
Why are you playing these childish games?
You had seemed so mature, now I'm not so sure.
I would be your object, if you'd proudly possess me.
Yet i feel that you would leave me forgotten,
in the lost and found.

Keep me warm

Cheyenne

Keep me warm
I'm scared of being left alone
surround me baby
shield me from the worlds wounds- so I can live in yours
I'll help heal you, my hands will help protect you from the cold
every breath from this chest will go towards keeping this fire
going
to keep you from freezing, and an attempt to defrost me from the pain that stuns me from growing old
that way we can gain wrinkles under our eyes, on our hands, and in our souls... together
every line an 'I love you' that we will never let go
because why erase our lives from our bodies to look young
when loves a mess, and every gray hair only means we hung on longer than most.

Peanut,
We will die one day, but I can only hope, pray and beg
that we will forever live with love, even though its marks leave our bodies as
battlefields, our hearts a pillow for our heads,

so when our lives get off course and the tempo of the world throws us off track
late at night, when we use our arms as blankets and our chests as confession booths,
the beating of our hearts will slow down our lives so we have a chance to get back on the right path

Handsome,
I know our stories going to be a hard one.
But that doesn't mean we shouldn't try
Distance is only an obstacle, but that doesn't hide the fact that when we slip from climbing it,
we only feel pain.
But I've felt worse. I know you have too.
So don't give up until you know that I'm not the one
Keep fighting for love as if it's all we have left because, baby, you will always be my only one
I'll give you my everything,
my body can only go so far; but for you I'd give up every last bone
for you too smooth down to use as skipping stones-
And when snow touches your skin and you become breathless,
take these lungs and use my air as your own-
And if the fire in my chest fails to keep you warm,
peel me, and use my skin as a coat
because it would be an honor to help cover you from the world

The Magic of Magic

George

I locked eyes with the beast! He stood a towering three feet higher than I at 5'11". Weighing in at a whopping 4000 pounds! I knew why they named him the monster… I walked to him and extended my arm in a friendly gesture only to be turned down. I knew at that moment he was no formidable opponent because he had already admitted defeat. I took to my side as did he. I was calm. He looked enraged with power and might coursing through his veins. With the ambiance of yelling, screaming, cheering, and stomping I knew it would be a good one. The man was ironically strong. He may be able to lift a couple tons of dead weight, his heart and mind were that of an infant. Still I was puzzled by him. I just couldn't understand his dedication and his ferocity.

I asked him "Why are you here?"

He boasted with arrogance "To win of course!"

He neglected to ask the same of me. So the match began. At first he had the advantage over me. I was startled by his haste. But we continued and the war waged on. In round one he had me no doubt, but I wanted him to think he had won. His own arrogance would be the downfall of his victory. Round 2 was about to begin and he still had no intention of having anything to do with me other than the match up. When he had beaten me even more efficiently in the second round I knew I would have to make my stand now. We stood face to face. Well as much as possible with a 3 foot difference.

I asked him "do you have any final words?"

He replied "final? Are you implying you're going to eliminate me in one round?"

"Yes," I said "unfortunately."

He walked to his side, I on mine. He looked baffled by what I had said to him. When the round started, he again had the advantage. Then it hit him. I swiftly played my final card, taking his great might and power, swiftly dethroning him.

"How!?" he cried.

I said "You never asked me why I was here."

"Then why?" he said.

"To show a man hiding from his own fears with his power what he should really be afraid of."

"And what's that?" He said

"The passion of a man with nothing left!" Then I walked away. On my way out he stopped me.

All he said was "thank you."

"What for" I asked.

"For reminding me how I got here". I said "No problem, friend" and never saw my best friend again.

Untitled

Brittney

Can't do anything right
Not sure where I'm supposed to find this light
This hole I'm in, it feels so tight
I already know I won't win this fight,
My faith is out of sight.
I feel my grip start to die,
But I only let out the occasional sigh,
And proceed with the lie.
People don't hear my endless plea
They just let me be
They believe that's the key
Sometimes, so do I.
But at night I ask why
peace of mind
Is so damn hard to find.
I ask myself why I am left with only air
And a body left bare
In the arms of someone who doesn't care.
I try not to compare.
But I wonder if this is fair,
But in truth or dare,
He never fails to choose dare,
So I feign to lose care
To the fact that he's never there.
But backwards my body still bends,

To him it is everything I send,
It's my heart that I lend
But the end is just pretend.
And when his lust truly descends,
There will be no honor left to defend.

Happiness

Chad

My pregnant eyes proofread my final message.
There is so much difficulty where there should be light.
How I long for our discourse while patiently accepting
reluctance.

Why should my hungers demand such weeping meals?
Desires deemed demented drive me toward that end.
Wherefore the joy I had must now be sad.
Oh my sad, sad soul severed so by masochistic
ambitions.
My heart has been rended for all the wonders I
intended.

I refuse to compete for my happiness.
I don't ask for much, but my happiness should be my
own.
I refuse to be first; my happiness will not be wrested
from another.
Yet I can not know satisfaction while perfection will
hear my words.
So I will know bliss while complements fail to
disappoint.

The Only Thing Worse

Cheyenne

LEFT HAND
I'm sitting here,
wrapped in the warmth
of a simple jacket you lent me
so I could walk home
and honestly without it I would've frozen

So it got me thinking,

Is this the definition of love?
Giving everything you can to make sure they stay warm
with their fingers intertwined with your own?
Because if that's the case I would give up these very
shoes,
and walk barefoot through the snow if it meant
your feet would keep dry.
If that's the case then,
I'd wait outside of every one of your classes,
that way if you got in trouble, I could tell you you're
stupid
and then hug you and apologize.
I'd collect every ray of sunlight in a jar,
that way I could fade into the background,
so you could shine brighter than the sun itself.
that way you could see that you're the only one I see

because you shine brighter than the rest of us.

I'd give up my body for you to use
as your personal pillow, your personal teddy bear, as
your personal toy
even if it means I have to get left behind at some point
when you grow up.

I'd be your umbrella for life
to shelter you from this world - and myself
because the only thing worse than a broken heart,
is two of them.

So I will give up my heart, and leave it beating at your
door.
and in fine print on the receipt (just in case you wanted
something more),
would be
not returnable if broken

RIGHT HAND
You are not him.
I remember waking up in the middle of the night,
because I used to sleep crying three words that I was too
scared to believe
you left me behind for a better tomorrow, without even
a goodbye -
and sometimes silence is the worst kind of pain.

I gave you my heart as an open canvas,
but instead of coloring inside of the lines,
you left me blank in the end,
only an incomplete sentence written on my heart
that I had to fill in so I didn't bleed the other words
I LO-
what meant to be I love you, turned to I loath you
but what I couldn't believe was that even after months of convincing myself
that I ruined it, that these tattered pages of my book of a mind
weren't good enough
I was still crying myself to sleep, with three words tattooed to the tip of my tongue,
I missed you.

But sometimes love isn't what's best for two people
and that's when I learned, the only thing worse than a broken heart,
is two.
I didn't know you were broken

We See What Isn't There

George

Colder than an arctic blast
No heat can warm that which isn't there
I try to put myself in place of this vacancy
Only to fall short like a man testing for pregnancy
You see not what is there only that which is not
The time I sacrifice will never span the physical gap of a
  collapsed bridge
Two seats on a swing-set with little breeze

And yet you have two faces
The other and unfamiliar side has an aggression
It comes shooting through my walls of compassion
As the sun to a plume of fog
So I paint it out for you
Only to have my colors melt off the page
Leaving nothing but another vacancy
But, never fear for I will brave the storms
For I can see your light shining through
Calling me to what is left inside that vacancy
Really you just can't see

The Bad Crowd

Rhiannin

Some people would say that I had fallen in with the 'wrong crowd'. By society's definitions, I suppose I had.

Friendship can be a hard thing to find, especially when you're odd. After years of oddness and bullying, of intolerance and expected cruelties it gets even harder. The things that have been said, thought, done to and about you carry down through the years. Each rumor compounds the others, each moment of hate feeds future hatreds. They all provide the fodder on which intolerance feeds. It is why some people are targeted relentlessly. We fall into a trap of expectance, accepting that this is the way it will be, the way it always will be. Acceptance becomes a habit. For those around us it can become a habit to bully, sometimes without reason or provocation needed.

Growing up in this situation, growing up the odd one, the bullied, it didn't take long for me to form exactly that habit. I pretended that it didn't bother me anymore. I put on a brave face and told myself not only that it didn't matter, but that because I had convinced myself it didn't matter, it would stop. This is what we're told from kindergarten on, right? Adults assure us that a policy of no reaction will eventually solve the problem. It doesn't.

Ironically, it was only after reaching this point that my longing for friendship, to fit in, to be allowed to be myself without being perpetually strange, came to it's peak. I didn't even know at the time, that I was longing for the very thing I told myself was perfectly acceptable.

You can imagine, then, the surprise of finding exactly such a place. More accurately I had found such a crowd. The wrong crowd.

I have never been, nor am I now, a druggie. I have never been arrested. I don't smoke. While living with my parents I didn't sneak out, I didn't cut classes, I turned in my homework on time (mostly). I also wore all black, longed to dye my hair outlandish colors, spent lunches alone or in the library, kept my nose perpetually in a book, and generally avoided people. Because of the way I acted and dressed, and because I did my best to keep my head down and avoid notice by my teachers and my peers, I was also growing accustomed to a generally poor reaction from strange adults, suspicion from teachers, and odd glances when I went out to public venues. Really, aside from my mood and feeling of exclusion, I didn't fit most of the stereotypes I was burdened with.

In 7th grade I was supposedly pregnant more than 10 times first semester alone. I was a virgin. Twice I was accused of soliciting money for sex, similar to Olive in *Easy A*, and because of this reputation it wasn't long before the boys in my school began sexually teasing me, groping me in the halls, and generally acting with zero regard for my personal boundaries or the truth.

Is it any wonder I fell in with the 'bad crowd?' They were the first people who accepted me, who didn't believe the rumors.

I'll admit that despite certain aesthetic similarities between myself and what was commonly known as the skater/goth crowd (a combination of the two, not a melding of the different styles), I was afraid. Here were the people who wore pretty much exactly what I wished I could (and no, they did not engage in slut-wear), had colorful hair, heavy eyeliner, smelled of cigarette smoke, and universally had either violent or slutty reputations. I didn't know then what a saving grace these people would become.

It wasn't until second semester that I found them. One of the few friends I did have suggested we sit at their table, and I think it must have been obvious how nervous I was. The girl sitting next to me made a point of joking with me, asking how my day had gone. Mostly they pretended not to notice my nerves, and even though I didn't join conversation that day, when I eventually did they accepted it with the ease and grace only people who truly understand social-fears can. Finally, I had found a place where people were open and honest not only about their opinions, but also about themselves. All they expected in return was that I do the same.

We all remember the summer that followed as the best summer of our school years.

There were about 25 of us, ranging in age from 12 to 24, who spent nearly every day of that summer lounging around a local gazebo. Cigarette smoke hung thick in the ceiling, laughter rang loud through the rest of the park, and occasionally silence settled comfortably into our bones. We chatted, played games, joked, and provided support (even when it was silent). The whole summer through we sweated in our black clothes, laughed at the rumors that had been told about us, and watched with amusement as passers-by stared with open revulsion.

Despite the fact that half the group were by that point chain-smokers, never once was I offered a cigarette. I have experienced more pressure to try drugs, to drink, in literally every other crowd. By about mid summer there were those so protective of me that they both threatened me to stay away from the cigarettes they themselves consumed (a bit of well-intended hypocrisy) and promised to protect me should I ever need it (many of my new friends were well acquainted with being 'jumped'). After finding out that I had in fact been stalked home by a much older man during the school year one of the older boys made sure to walk me, and a couple other girls who went to the same middle-school, home most days.

I was safe. I was loved. These people became my family. And regardless of what they did with their evenings, no matter how many drugs they used, or if they had a criminal record, not one of them advocated the kind of misbehavior so commonly associated with them.

Honestly, the reason so many of them smoked, the reason they used drugs, the reason they cut, the reason they acted out, wasn't because they were bad kids. It was because they were the odd ones, the ones that didn't fit in, the ones who fell victim to the snowball effect of bullying so often it had become an avalanche, and because no one had been there to help them.

The 'bad crowd' saved me. Some days literally.

It never happened again. No one spent time at the gazebo the next summer, nor had they ever in the summers before. People moved away, got jobs, lives changed, and so did friendships. We all found new interests, most found new friends, new families; the summer had passed. But we all remember it. When we run into each other we all talk about it.

I guess I don't know what matters more: realizing that people who do 'bad kid' things aren't necessarily bad people, or realizing the impact of bullying, or realizing the importance of friendship, or maybe just looking into the head of one lonely kid who was scooped up and set on a path she couldn't have reached on her own. But all those things have something in common - you don't know what you're looking at until you look deeper. The surface is a lie, especially the surface portrayed by the media, by the school, by the biases and the hate.

They were my friends. They smoked cigarettes, they were druggies, they cut, and many of them had attempted suicide. They were also the kindest people I have ever met. They were the most willing to love, the most eager to be loved. They were generous, protective, fiercely loyal. They were themselves. We were ourselves. How many middle school kids can say that?

Commentary

I've always known it's not right to judge by appearance or stereotypes. Nevertheless, it was an eye-opening moment when I read this piece and learned that people with bad reputations, people who cut, or smoke, or drink, or any of the other negative stereotypes society has, aren't necessarily "bad" people. It made me think about the way we apply stereotypes to those around us. We all do it, or have done it at one time or another. I do it all the time, without thinking about it. But this essay made me stop and wonder if maybe those stereotypes I apply so quickly aren't true, or aren't true all the way through.

If I see a girl with lots of straps on her shoulders, dangling earrings, and a cellphone, chatting with a friend, I tend to dismiss her as "One of Them", one of those strange creatures known as a "public-schooled teenage girl" who does who-knows-what with who-knows-whom and thinks purely of her reflection and social status, and has nothing better to do than giggle, complain, and hang out with her questionable boyfriend.

But I don't know this girl. I don't know that she's not bullied, or perhaps cares for a younger brother or sister. Maybe she supports charity work, or has to deal with her parents' divorce. I know nothing about her. Is it fair to judge her by my stereotype based on her appearance?

When the public-schooled kids at Youth Group passed on rumors surrounding various individuals at their school, I shuddered (like the sheltered homeschooler I am) and assumed the rumors were true. I never dreamed an innocent girl could have the reputation of a slut. If a girl (or boy) had a bad reputation, I assumed it was true. I didn't know what damage believing a rumor could do.

Now, because I've read "The Bad Crowd", I try to think twice before I judge someone based on their appearance, and I'm more reluctant to accept what public rumor has to say about them. I think about this piece, and how the "Bad Crowd", the one everyone avoided, was in fact the most loving crowd, the most caring crowd, and the crowd most in need of being loved by others.

Will you?

- Megan

Summer of Friendship

Megan

There are so many friends upon our street,
They always want to hang out and to play.
No other company could be as sweet,
As friendship shared in such a friendly way.

We run, we build, we laugh and sometimes cry,
As summer winds her way towards the fall.
We gather round and together we sigh,
Unwilling to answer the season's call.

But while sun shines I'll play with great relief,
Enjoying golden days as they will come,
For now it is my very firm belief,
Since golden days swift turn from some to none,

Each day to me invaluable shall be,
Forever living in my memory.

Commentary

This was written two years ago as a part of a poetry class. Our teacher had just introduced us to the Shakespearean sonnet form and I couldn't wait to try it out. Foremost in my mind at the time were the incredible blessings of a Friendship Summer. We were friends with almost all of the families on our street, and around 3-4pm people would start to come out of their houses. We spent every evening in someone's garage or backyard, laughing with the adults, playing with the kids and reveling in every moment of it. It was extra special because that spring I had finally figured out how to turn off the "voice" which tells me what I could be doing or should be doing, and stay in the moment, "for these times are golden and will not come again."

- Megan

Summary

David Romig

This chapter does remind us that "no man is an island unto himself" as we are touched and moved by our relationships with others for good or for ill. How we then choose to respond to the behaviors of others makes us who we are in the eyes of others and even ourselves. How will we respond, indeed will we respond to our youth? The words written here by our youth show what a strong impact for good or for ill their experiences may be, in part, due to fewer life experiences. So, as Chad says in "How I Feel in 90 Words," will we complain and complain and do nothing to change, or do we choose to really listen and learn from what they are sharing with us. The pains and the joys can seem so much more intense, the bullies and the friendships, too. Will we be there to help and support our youth, as they go through these experiences.

I can remember my sister when she broke up with her first serious boyfriend. She seemed convinced that her life was over, but for her, there was the support of friends and family to help her through it. Not every youth has such support systems, and while these days, artificially, we may appear more connected than ever with social media, many youth feel extremely isolated, alone, and uncared for. Today, suicide among teenagers and young adults continues to be a significant problem. In, "Keep me Warm," Cheyenne reminds us how scary it can be to feel isolated and alone and how important it is to feel protected and cared for. So, will we make ourselves available to our youth, or will we stay away hiding from our own fears, as the adversary did in George's, "The Magic of Magic". In a time of need, we can choose to be there to help and support our youth.

We can learn from them too. Maybe "The Bad Crowd" isn't so bad after all, as Rhiannin's shares. We need to stop judging our youth when we really do not know or understand what they are actually going through. Only they can tell us. They can also share and remind us of the good times, as Megan did with, "Summer of Friendship." I can remember my own summer days in high school and college when my friends and I still saw the world as new, and we felt that we would go out and change the world. Maybe we did in some small ways, and maybe we still can, if we choose and if we listen.

On Becoming

Relationships, significant life events, the world around us are all part of the equation that describes us, each as an individual. Or at least we like to think so. But life is not so simple - people can't be reduced to equations, no matter how complex. Being described by an equation implies that we have reached some predictable pattern or line that describes us. Perhaps we like to think of ourselves as constant and predictable.

Then something happens to change that perspective. There is a discontinuity in our equation. It may be a great love we want to experience, and we change to do so. Or, it may be a cataclysmic event that requires us to "rise above" in order to survive. Some might say it is the randomness of the universe, others fate. Whatever the source, our humanity is always challenged and often must adapt in order to continue.

It is a constant battle. We are always trying to meet the unexpected, the challenges. It requires that we constantly adapt in some way. Adaptation equals change. Change means that we are always becoming. Indeed, always becoming is the same thing as growing; the process of adapting to changing conditions in order to survive. When we stop becoming, we die.

But what does that process of constantly becoming look like? It is different for each of us. And as we grow older, we try to resist that process. Change is hard. Still, to live we must change. Sometimes we need to be reminded what constantly "becoming" looks like.

- Eric Smith

The End of Something Beautiful

Cheyenne

It started at the end of something beautiful,
and because of that it made it the hardest part to deal,
Knowing something so precious to my heart
Could so easily kill.
Who would've known that it would be my beautiful
insanity that would
make my world end in an uneasy clarity.

My odd dreams of the ocean being my sky,
turning into the very thing that drowned me in the end,
head under water,
heart above the clouds,
when my heart was shot down,
is when I came to the realization that the world is round,
and that you walking to each corner of my square
imagination
would never happen.
It started with a pinky promise, and ended with us
growing up.

How

Brittney

How do you survive,
When you don't wish to be alive.
Why would you strive,
When all you're getting is painful vibes, hearing cries and lies, and watching the world die.
The world is on fire we're caught up in desire
We want, want, want, and take more than we can get and share nothing at all because truly no one cares, in their eyes there's no one there.
People stop and stare, and judge you for what it is that their ignorance just missed.
The barrier exists between every name on the list.
Kisses, and fists, disses, and strange abyss.
We don't know who we are, or even where we came from.

Its hard to carry on when you know one day you'll be gone anyway.
They tell you to stay strong and it wont be long until happiness comes along, but everyone is wrong.
For happiness is a faith, a religion, a belief, perhaps even a myth.
Faith is cast upon us and they act like it will last.
We're walking through this maze with the walls closing in. The haze that we face simply puts us in a daze.

They say its just a phase
Perhaps I'm a little crazed.
But you'd be quite amazed...

World of Insanity

Rhiannin

There is a place in time
Where only we can be
And when I close my eyes
It's just you and me
I'm not asking you to save me
Just stand by me
While I free myself
From the chains of this world of confusion!

I know it's mad
The past that still haunts
Our darkened eyes and minds
But between us I think
We can see past the melancholy dreams
Of a world tossed into insanity
Only we can be,
In this place and time
Between the worlds of reality and rhyme
All I ask all I need
Is someone to stand by me
As I free myself from the chains

of this world of confusion
Consumed we've been before
Lost to the sands of time,

Our heads drawn through time
by a chariot as we run behind
The darkness growing in our minds
Tripped we've been
And left out alone in the cold

Without the light of a future

by which to warm our bones

I'm not asking you to save me from the darkness we've
seen
All I need is someone to stand by me
As I set myself free from the chains
of this world of confusion!
Watch!
Breathe!
Stand! Stand by me,
As we set ourselves free
From the chains of this world of confusion!
No matter how many they may be,
Or how often they draw us back,
I'll set myself free!
Watch as we free ourselves from this insanity!

In the Dirt

Cheyenne

I'm beginning to feel like a joke
what do you do when you hate something so much that you start hating yourself?
it's like trying to put your foot into a shoe that doesn't fit,
so you walk around with your toes curled because there is no room to slide around.
Yet I continue do it because it makes me look good,
because four more inches is like four more possibilities of being noticed-
even if the shoe doesn't fit.

Take notice,
I'm too scared to walk into a crowd and shout my own name out because I have to do it alone,
but I'm too proud to step down off of the chair I've pulled out because someone told me to kill myself.
Its not that I'm suicidal, just too stubborn to ignore them instead of saying
"Don't think I will? Watch me."
My very own dreams and ambitions becoming the noose I've been getting a rope burn from.
So tell me, what am I suppose to do when Disney channel makes having babies look so fun,
yet the moment I think about dropping out, suddenly I'm the one the world looks down on

I think that's so fucked up, shouldn't it be the other way
around?
smarter than 75 percent of my peers, yet perceived as
the dumb one.
Haven't they once thought that maybe I stopped caring
because they all cared too much?

I'm beginning to feel like a joke
I've been told more than once "well have you considered
a career in writing?"
but I don't think they understand that's what I'm
currently doing
I don't need to be paid to have a job that I love pursuing
I just need to be heard.
But then again, a few head nods and "good job" 's isn't
going to pay the bills.

So is what I'm doing really that wrong?
Or am iIust the typical teenage rebel who needs to keep
her nose down in the dirt
because its better to do what I'm told instead of going
out and making this life my own-
Should I not get the choice to because I'm too young?
I'm beginning to feel like a joke

Thunder

Rhiannin

I need somewhere tall
And far away,
Where nothing but the clouds
Can hear the things I'd say.
I'd need a place far past the
Realm of locks and keys
Because whispered words
are too oft overheard,
And words meant for private ears alone
Have a way of traveling
Out into the world
On their own.

Secrets are better kept
When not kept at all
For untold
Burn shining holes
In those that touch them, true.
But trust not can I
The listening ears around
For those who'd hear me
Do not revere the sound
And speak too freely.

Some things

Though secret not,
Ought not be told -
save to the clouds.
Atop some mountain
Fair and far,
Above the flights of birds,
T'is here alone I'll vent my woe
And the secrets I've been told.
Where none will hear the verse I've written.
Because perhaps the clouds
Can riotously unburden
The things I cannot.

For who would justly fear
The anger of a youth,
Or a girl?
When words like angst
Exist to dull and parry it?
And who would trust the things I speak
When age, debt, and culture's ways
Have yet to gag my thought?

But who would Dare deny,
A Storm-Cloud in a tantrum?
Yell back at Thunder's booming
Condemnation?
I think not.

The Iron Heart

George

One foot forward two legs back
Everyone says you kids only know how to rap.
Well let me tell you some of us are lying on our back
Choking on society and its harsh medicine crap.
No don't step there, no don't speak now.
If I'm not stepping there, then where, and how?

Don't speak now, you say, yet you're the ideological hypocrite.
Blood is red and ink is blue yet sometimes I'm writing with the two.
Love is black and happiness green, yet I'm forced to believe they're not on opposite sides of the color scheme.
What's my problem? The fact that you don't have one.
Put innocence in and get revenge out,
My guts are turning them selves in because they know what they want is only a crime yet to be committed.
Just be positive they say, but all I'm really positive about is that they make emotions into wood
Only meant to be built into my monument of "good"
What is good when "bad" feels right and that good is burning over my low hood?
But I'll stand tall, because no iron heart can get truly burned.

When that poor kid comes running in you'll be the one to turn them down again

"I'm counting to three!" "Oh no!, now he's waiting for me" Secondary treatment was agreed.
But I'll be waiting at the end.
So maybe my answer doesn't follow your trend.
Does that justify me living by your parameters just 'cause you got scarred?
Secondary treatment isn't what they deserve. In the old days that was called absurd.
Life grabs you by the feet when you're barely treading water
And it's only in those last seconds that you'll ever realize it's time to bring this shit to an end.

Ugly

Rhiannin

When I was a little girl
There was no such thing as ugly...
We were all Disney cartoons
Pen and paper princesses
And though my models of perfection
Were a confection of cheap plastic

I could not see that

Maybe the girl next to me
Was never going to be
Beauty.
I couldn't imagine that ugly
Would not be like the Beast,
And that the touch of
One of my plastic princesses
Could not change that facade

Back then I'd never looked at the models on a magazine
Or stared up at an actress and wished that she was me
My pretends were just games,
And though I played Cinderella and Sleeping Beauty
When I went to sleep it was okay to just be me...

You see, when I was a little girl

I did not think
That by the time my
Indoctrination was complete
I'd be so caught up in the lies
And twisting my tortured body
Into a metallic frame
I didn't imagine that the color of my lips
Would daily require painting
Or that I'd struggle to look like Barbie
Though the harsh reality
Would be that if I saw her standing before me
I'd doubtless be sickened

When I was a little girl I didn't know
That showing skin was not an option
But a required law of life

I did not know that if a man raped me
He'd probably blame me

I didn't know that I could grow up
With plain hair, or dull eyes
I couldn't imagine
A world in which my personality
Was so far down on the list of quality
That I'd starve my living body
Just to fit the mold
Or that each day I'd paint a new face over the old.

I didn't know that this world twisted and tortured girls
I did not know that all they wanted me to be
Was a toy no more real than my plastic Barbie

Fuck this reality
Because there's no way that a girl that believed in the
power of her princesses
Will sell her soul to this devilish conspiracy,
This body is not for sale!
This mind cannot be bought!
My beauty is my own
No matter what you thought
I don't owe you anything!
I'm not your window dressing!
My perfection is my own,
Anything but plastic.

Words

Chad

the weight of the words is intolerable
line after line constricting unfathomable
each sentence holding me fast
by my overambitious past
I fall on page after page
kept up in this haze belying an age
if I could free myself from this cage
I would be beyond my gaze
with so much freedom to build my haze

A Plea

Cheyenne

Help me.
I'm crying out
I fucking can't stand myself
Living in a body that doesn't want me,
like forcing your foot into a shoe that doesn't fit
no wiggle room, just toes curled
and I've done nothing but hurt myself because of it

Fucking help me.
I'm gasping for air,
but these bandages covering my body are keeping me
    suffocated
every cut another chance to breathe
told "You aren't mentally well"
why can't I touch my own body when the world's hands
    can harm me
by sticking a needle into my arm to make me healthy?

Help. Me.
I've managed to get trapped in myself,
and I'm drowning because of it
that's what happens when I can't break through the
    surface
who would've though the skin I was born with would kill

What We Can Be

George

You would think that a 9 year old boy in a small town would have nothing to worry about, right? If you think so, you would be wrong. At 9 years old I was told, dead in the face with no space to breathe, that I had a life changing disease called diabetes. My family and I were destroyed by this and there was no proper health care for me. This was a tragedy.

Now 5 almost 6 years later I'm still alive, but I have turned into a different person than I would have been otherwise. I have learned that you should cherish every one's rights, beliefs, and lives. Most people are too concerned with money or something they would rather be doing to see that life is slowly slipping away. They have fought no real challenges or battles to make them stronger, they only think about selfish opportunities and ideas. I have a challenge to remind me every day that I can't waste time avoiding things that might be hard or a scary thought, and facing these make me stronger as a person.

But pushing back and challenging the fact that I may die before most of my friends, and that I could die any day, is what makes me stronger, making it possible for me to push again tomorrow and the next day. I did not expect this kind of challenge when I was 9 years old, nor did I fully understand what it meant for me. Sometimes life will give you the short stick, but that just forces you to be a better person than you thought you would be. When I was around 10 years old I almost went into a coma but I didn't, and I have never come close since. It was the moment in my life that I was truly showed the chances I could be losing. If we battle every challenge we face, it can only make us stronger to live another day.

We will always have battles to be fought. Whether or not we choose to fight them will shape us as a person. You can always tell the difference between a selfless leader and a deprived, fear-driven person. A selfless leader is someone who is brave and willing to fight for others, and pick you up when you can't hold your own weight. Someone who chooses not to stand up for themselves or others and runs at the sight of a challenge and cowers when a fight comes will never change or be proud of themselves when they look back at the opportunities they chose to avoid.

The best people in the world are, and always will be, people who chose to fight their challenges and not give in when it became scary or when it became irksome. They simply knew that they would keep fighting till they could no longer hold themselves up under the weight of their burdens. They are the people we remember the most. Like our founding fathers, Abraham Lincoln, Albert Einstein, or Nikola Tesla. These are the people that will never be forgotten because they fought for others and themselves.

When we become great, it is not because we got lucky or because we ran away. I believe when we persevere and never give in to our challenges, we will become as great as we can perceive ourselves to be.

Summary

Megan Houghton

Of this entire book, this chapter stood out the most to me. I can only do so much to summarize what these young men and women said because so much of it meant such a great deal. Our youth are experiencing the same tragedies as adults, yet they are trying to make sense of them for the first time. They feel alone, since too many adults write off their problems as "teenage angst". Yet, some of them are facing things most adults couldn't imagine, like George shows us in What We Can Be.

Many people avoid the topic of suicide because it's uncomfortable. However, depression, suicide, and poor self-esteem are major issues among young adults. Our youth are trying to figure out who they are. If we ignore these feelings, they may never figure it out. I think World of Insanity gives the best advice. We don't need to "fix" our youth, we need to genuinely support them. Encourage them to make solutions. Let them be their beautiful selves, regardless of what their version of beauty is. And, we need to help them when they ask for it, or when safety is concerned. The best saying I have ever heard is "Give them a safe environment to fail". Let them do their thing their way, within safe reason. And as Rhiannin told us, stand by them.

Faith

Today, when we talk about faith, we usually mean Faith with a capital F. That kind of faith is equated with a belief in God (whatever you call a supreme being) and any number of belief systems. Until the middle of the 20th century, in the US, that usually meant some form of Christianity. Since the 1960's the definition and use of the term Faith has become confused both with a long list of religions and with the concept of religion. When asked about our faith, we usually identify our religion, if we identify with one. But religion is not faith, it is a formal belief system. Today, many people do not grow up within the formal belief system of a specific religion. Is it any wonder, then, that people have trouble with faith, even as they search for it.

So what is faith, if not religion? A dictionary indicates faith is belief and trust in something or someone, even with no evidence the belief is well placed. Deity is not required. People or natural phenomena can be the objects of faith. Given that, faith is different for everyone.

But is faith necessary? It seems to be. All people seek something they can believe in, to have faith about. It seems to be part of the human condition. Often it takes the form of faith in a "greater power," but not always - ask any atheist. Still we seek. And in our contemporary life, filled with rapid changes and technological wonders, it is easy to become overwhelmed without the anchor of some kind of faith. But what does faith look like? How do we know if we have it? Those questions may not have simple answers, but looking at them through the eyes of our youth may help us clarify our own vision and definitions.

- Eric Smith

A Man and His Castle

Chad

i saw a man at a castle once.
He stood there in a strange way
As if to penetrate its wall with language.
He seemed foolishly obsessed with this princess,
who may have been inside but no one could say for certain.

You could say
i was that man.
However, it seems to Me
A decided lack of men
Can be observed
Among the women
Outside the walls of My castle.
Surely one of them
Would oblige Themselves
to the requittence of my language.

Why then must i sit below my ramparts,
So set upon my challenge
as i would call it?
it is only ourselves
we can so thoroughly deceive
into putting ones whole faith into a concept
Unless your profession

should be preacher or missionary.
Men will believe what they want
to believe. i suppose.

----

i would like to believe otherwise now...
Let us see whether or not
My previous determination
And desires can be overcome
By newer yearns for success

Commentary

I really thought hard about this piece and what it meant to me. At first I thought people are ignorant and faith will be foolish and determined without observation. The alternative being that the faith is not their own and that I think is even more foolish. That's when it hit me. A man AND his castle, it's not just a man. The castle plays a much bigger role than we give it credit for. Men see a pink castle and crowd around for the beautiful princess to look out her window. Who's to say the castle isn't black on the inside; Housing a knight of death and bloodshed. The knight believes his castle is black and the people are waiting for him to rain down upon them. But, the part that kills me is that when the knight finally leaves his castle the people outside still believe it's the princess, only to be slaughtered in their ignorance.

- George

Sermon

Chad

It is a safe assumption to make that Jesus did nothing unintentionally. When He appeared to the disciples, He knew that Thomas was not among them. Jesus knew that Thomas would not believe the other disciples when they told Thomas they had seen Jesus. Jesus can often teach a lesson when he does things like this.

Thomas did not react to the disciples' news much differently from how the disciples reacted to the news given to them by Mary. Before Jesus appeared before His disciples, they all doubted his resurrection.

After Jesus appeared to his disciples, they were given a chance to see from a different perspective how they acted when they spoke with Thomas; however, to chastise Thomas for his doubts of the disciples' declarations of their risen Lord would be hypocrisy, for the other disciples were just as guilty of doubting the good news. This event was a wonderful lesson for the disciples, so that they might understand the stubbornness of man better as they witnessed to the world, but it is also a lesson for us.

When Jesus speaks with Thomas, He says, "Blessed are they who have not seen, and yet still come to believe." Everyone in that scene has seen Jesus, so he is not blessing any of them. Jesus is speaking to his disciples, but he is also speaking to us. Jesus is blessing us, and we are blessed in our beliefs.

Several generations down the line, we must wait until Judgment day to see our savior for the first time. The disciples show us how hard it can be to have that faith, and if they had trouble then, we have it harder. How could we expect anyone today to have faith? Yet we are blessed with the capacity for faith, and for that we should be thankful.

Helpless

Cheyenne

I am lost
and need found
these shackles keep me
from leaving this ground
I want to move-
but I just can't seem to do it myself
help me, I'm helpless,
I need your help.

Undo these shackles I put onto my being
so I can thank you,
wave you off,
and secure them back on these
feet,
and watch as time makes iron rust,
and cut into tender feelings.
I want to leave,

I want to be free,
but I am helpless-
I need you to help me
help, please, I can't stop
from trapping myself.

Faith?

Rhiannin

Faith is a tricky word. In this country, today, the word Faith comes laden with extra meaning. Faith means Christianity, in one of its many forms, a belief in God. More over, to say that one has Faith seems to be even stronger than simply saying that one is religious, another word which, in a Christian-dominated country comes with the meaning of Christianity. Tricky words indeed for an individual who both considers herself religious, filled with faith, and yet is not Christian.

When forced to put a label to my beliefs I call myself Pagan, a term which is frequently used to mean anything which isn't one of the major religions, or else certain brands of non-religion. When people think 'pagan' they tend toward either modern day Wiccans and similar brands of faith, or else of ancient Celtic peoples, those termed 'witches' by common understanding of the middle ages and earlier European history. The term pagan, however, can also be applied to the Greek religion, now called mythology, as well as the Roman equivalent. It is a good term for most any ancient pre-monotheistic religion, although in some cases technically incorrect, it is a general enough word that most people understand what you mean without really understanding any specifics.

For me, in a Christian country, this is about as much as I want people to know at first. Certainly I have been asked, and am willing to explain, about the specifics of my own personal beliefs, but one of the first things I must explain is that these religions are perhaps most unified in that there are no two people who believe in the same way. Me explaining my religious belief is not like someone relating a key concept of the Bible. Not only is it unlikely that another person will agree completely with my concept and faith, it is entirely possible that someone who labels her/him self in the exact same way I do would find my belief totally incorrect and wrong. Fortunately, as I answer to no one but myself in my faith, I don't have to worry about anyone else claiming I am blasphemous or incorrect. Their opinions and arguments may affect me, or they may not, at my discretion, with no higher earthly power to answer to either way.

I explain this simply because I have, over the course of my life, realized how foreign this seems to many of my country men. Even the non-religious have a closely held concept of religion which is based on Christianity and, all too often, on the most extreme and therefore public branches thereof. That a concept of a religion which, while outwardly similar, may have nothing in common and no common core of belief, seems alien. It is perhaps ironic then that I, in turn, see large swaths of Christianity as equally foreign and strange.

For a moment, imagine that you entered a classroom with no knowledge of the bible, were never told bible stories growing up, had never known that Christmas was a celebration of Jesus' birthday, nor Easter the resurrection. You have never attended a church service, were never baptized, you know no bible verses. How much of your day, especially in school, is now missing?

If you couldn't imagine it really, I don't blame you. For most the influence is innocuous. Yet, imagine getting through a high school or college level English course with no understanding of Bible references until someone tells you what they are and explains the story/verse/etc. This is my school career. If I wish to say the Pledge of Allegiance I must pay homage to a religion not my own. In politics I am constantly faced with politicians who represent the beliefs of their religion as the beliefs the country must uphold, solely because that religion calls for us to do so, when that religion is not my own. In conversations I have utterly missed references, applying them in some other way, until someone explained that it was a bible reference.

Now, I am not trying to say that this is a bad thing. While I certainly disagree with the penetration of Christian doctrine in some aspects of our society, this is more due to a disagreement over rights than any disagreement over ideas or values. Namely my right as a Untied States citizen to practice and live by a different set of ideals. Often those ideals are so close to identical it makes no difference.

What I am attempting to call to attention is the inundation of this belief. Christianity is so powerful that it influences the lives of thousands of non-Christian individuals, if not millions, within our borders and without. When words like Faith and Religion are burdened by so specific a meaning, what can it possibly mean for those who employ the word without it's societal connotation? I am a woman of Faith. I am a Religious woman. I am a religious woman living in a society which, on one level or another thinks that I am wrong, that I should not use that word in that way, and that I am without faith simply because I am without Christian faith. Yet, the Christians I have encountered, whom I admire the most, all advocate for the same personal relationship, the same personal responsibility in faith which is so critical to my form of paganism. Certainly we disagree in specifics of some things, but the center is remarkably similar.

Is Faith what you believe in, or is it the act and emotion of Belief? Is Religion personal, public, or societal? These are questions our country has answered in one way, and treated in another. These a questions which demand a true answer, not the current ambiguity.

Will We Listen ?

Faith in 42

George

What if I told you that when I wake up in the morning
I'm not happy?
I sit up slowly and again realize the people I want to see
aren't standing around me.

What if I told you the thing you desire most is out of
reach?
Would it cause you to test the self detrimental
limitations of your own boundaries?

I would think that the answers to "life, the universe, and
everything" would be right next to me
Only to end up searching for that which is creating self
limiting boundaries to keep me from realizing that
things around me don't add up to 42.
No, they only add up to me and you.

The desire to proclaim your own view is only
predetermining that the choice still isn't up to you.
The choice of whether to see or do, to not self-contain
that which is truly you
but we question not ourselves as we are the ignorant
prodigies of those whom we never really knew.
Pretending to be the likes of whom only god's son
himself could merely dream to be, silence our own

doubts as though he should be righteous right out of the womb.

Take a breath now for those who died before you, but what's the point if they don't even know you?

We try to lie as our sons and daughters pick up on the clues' as they pierce the sheet which hangs in the fore-view to quickly see light before the guillotine slices the reflective innocence allowing them to see true.
We teach our selves not to because we are afraid of what we could do, to say we have power, and turn it into voodoo.

They cripple the remaining soldiers because it was not enough to make it through the war, but because we said we would die, that makes it what we should do.

I refuse to believe we have a clear view of our life, the tip of our nose is the only light to guide us by night into that which we can only describe as fright!

We do not get advice, not even a simple cue of when it is our turn to step onto the stage, that is our own mind determining what we could do, but instead we guess. Jump early and you'll end up preaching to those that can't hear you, step up late and they all want to kill you!

We fool ourselves by saying that the person next to you will willingly be used like a pool cue to knock your idea into the next causing a chain reaction of good hue.

You reach out and grab the hand next to you because you don't know who will be the next to sink into the great blue and those who refuse fall without even the chance of good fortune.

So I say to myself why is it that I even pretend to see you and I come to the conclusion that it's the only hope I have to make it through. So when I call out for those that are willing to see anew, I can only hope it will be me and you adding up to 42.

Faith

Chad

How ever can I
Persist and always
deny
The struggles that go
by.
While I wonder why
I even try.
When all seems nigh
And my thoughts drift
high,
In the clouded sky,
Where a future I spy
Is disastrously dry.
So I ask myself why
I even try,
While inwardly I deny
That everything will
be fine

Is it that i am cursed
With this stigma so
obsessed
That i can be
distracted from
my conquest
Over that ever so
abscessed
And perpetually
perceived
success?
The prey i have
stalked i can
never possess.
For the sum of all
things is to be
detested
By the best of what's
left in the rest
of our souls,
If only our goals could
be accomplished
by less
than man's favored
goddess.

Summary

Eric

This chapter is a challenge. There is so much diversity among the pieces that a summary seems like a repeat and just as long. But the real challenge is to my thinking, my notions of faith as I experience it. Chad and George begin by questioning faith as something both consuming and potentially deceptive. Through faith, we see things, not as they are, but as we want them to be. And often what we want colors our view of what actually is, resulting in our not really accepting or dealing with reality as it is. A parent shows signs of dementia or a teen shows signs of self-harm, but we believe "it can't happen in our family" and so our faith causes us to miss the signs until they become too overwhelming. Then, not only do we have to deal with reality, but we have to question our own faith.

Does that mean faith is bad? No! Consider the lesson of Timothy in Sermon. Blessed are those who have not seen and still believe. There is value in having faith, even as we deal with sometimes challenging reality. Faith that someone is there or that things will be better can be very comforting and can help us get through difficult times.

Sometimes though, especially when we are young, we find ourselves needing that faith anchor and don't have it. Many today do not grow up with a spiritual foundation. Maybe their parents rebelled against the "strict rules" they experienced. Or maybe they wanted their children to define faith for themselves, but provided little experience to build upon. Regardless, many feel the need for help, for something to believe in that is beyond themselves. They feel Helpless and in need.

But what if you have a faith, though it is not the same as your peers? That, too, becomes complicated because having a faith that is different may be perceived as wrong, even dangerous. Further, when faith and religion are confused, people often begin to think that their religion makes them superior and that everyone must believe the way their religion dictates. In turn this leads to discrimination, even dehumanization – just look at all of the "so called" religion-based conflicts around the world. Even something as simple as saying the Pledge of Allegiance can cause difficulty for someone with different beliefs. Is it right for us to judge, to force someone to become something other than what they believe? Why can't we accept people and their beliefs and learn through sharing?

Perhaps we should look at things another way. That is what Faith in 42 suggests. Maybe in the end, it comes down to finding a way to build community, one person at a time, and together finding a path built by adding our beliefs together. And when we do, the result is the answer to the ultimate question, 42 to borrow from Douglas Adams.

All of this is wonderful philosophical discussion but in the end, it comes down to faith is needed and desired, yet is difficult to find. Once found, we face other challenges that mostly have to do with somehow living with each other in positive ways rather than trying to destroy each other simply because we are different.

Finding Our Voice

Have you ever had a great idea or critical insight and when you tried to share it, no one listened? It is an experience most of us have had. None of us command attention all of the time. And when we are not able to express our insights and ideas, we become frustrated. If it happens enough, we may even give up, leave the group or scene, and try to find one more suitable, where others will allow us to exercise our Voice.

But to exercise our Voice, we must first find it. Then when found, sometimes while finding, we have to find or make a path or place where that Voice can be heard. Sometimes it is easy - our friends are likely to listen. But when we want our Voice to have an impact beyond our inner circle, we need to somehow pave the way. Or find someone to pave it for us. We have to be seen as credible and knowledgeable. Without that, no one will listen to our Voice, no matter how polished, reasoned, or loud.

If you are young, your challenge is greater still. You are growing and evolving rapidly. So you struggle to find what you value enough to raise your Voice. At the same time, you are young and society often equates young with being unable to form and support an opinion. Even when young people are seen as having passion and opinions, those opinions are discounted - alter all, they can't be old enough to have valid Voices yet.

But it isn't true! Often, young people see things we miss, because they are young, that are important. Listen as our youth seek their own voices and share both the struggle and the passion, even wisdom. What might we learn about ourselves, if we would only listen to those Voices?

- Eric Smith

Ink

Rhiannin

Who cares for the youthful young poet,
Unnamed and unknown,
Sitting in his room all alone?

Who cares for the words that he's written
On crisp printing page,
All for the sake of his lack of an age?

What he says is the truth, burning fast burning true
Blinded mind racing,
To send pencil and pen, raving across the paper so that
then
The words of the voices boiling 'round
The thought, feelings, sensations and sound
Can be recorded in truth,
The power, the vision, the crime, the youth.

Though the muses are playing in his mind,
loud as an organ,
Unstoppable,
without time,
And the words they give him are righteous,
and the pages he's written are not printed with words
but with truth,
And the ink flowing soft from his pen,

Is not ink,
It's the blood that he's spent,
Facing the world with his truths and his lies,
And always,
Always,
Being denied.

For who cares for the poet,
sitting alone in darkened room?
His importance bows
To the one in his tomb.

In the world there are few unquestionable truths.
How can we afford to lose
Those recorded in the voice of the youth?

Commentary

Before I try to make any grand meaning out of this poem I have to admit, Ink is essentially a poem born of angst and irritation. An expression of my own lack of a voice, Ink is entirely about being voiceless.

Youth, while a critical point, and my no means one I want to discredit, is really only one aspect of a larger problem. Basically, it's a reflection on 'not in my backyard' syndrome applied to anyone better than average. Which isn't me trying to say that I am above average, its more trying to understand why we value the things we do in the moment, and yet so many of the people we see as great, generations later, were unknown or known and belittled and ignored in their own time. Most importantly it's my way of trying to tell people that we're still doing it!

Youth is really subjective here. I mostly mean that we, as a society, tend to ignore people until they reach a certain age and maturity level despite experience, maturity, or apparent wisdom. The truly remarkable have time and again [dis]proven this assumption about age increasing one's capacity for greatness. Malala Yousafzai is an incredible example of a very young individual being absolutely awe-inspiring. And she is but one example of a young person who exceeds the expectations placed on her, and on her peers, in incredible and seemingly impossible ways. The fact of the matter is, while individuals like Malala are rare, the spark of wisdom, courage, and greatness, which allows her to be and do the things she has, is not. It's simply uncomfortable to have that kind of thing in your backyard. We all want to be special and unique. And, it's infinitely harder to think of yourself as a real diamond of humanity when you are faced with someone who has even a tiny portion of truth you don't, even if you have a tiny portion of truth they don't. So, while youth is mostly a reflection of the age expectations in society, it is also largely meant to be anyone still alive. For me, Ink is about silencing truth because of it's source, or because it is hard to swallow. Ink is about society's habit of silencing great truths.

- Rhiannin

Music

Megan

The music flows through me,
Tells me how to move,
Where to leap, where to turn.

Music.

The language of the soul itself,
Too pure for words,
It sings straight to the soul.
No words, no rules,
Just heart-to-heart
Communication.
Sounds of tears,
Leaps of joy,
The shrill pain of a broken heart,
The hope of a new dawn.

Music.

Commentary

I would not generally classify myself as a "music person", but I continue to be amazed by the power of this medium. You can listen to a piece of music by someone completely different from you, and yet you understand it, just by the sound. We can distinguish a lament from a song of victory, even if we don't "speak" this language ourselves. We can still be carried away by it.

Deleted Lines (Like deleted scenes, only in writing)

The only purer language is God's Love.

This was the original last line of the poem (it came after the last "Music"), but when we looked at it critically, I realized (reluctantly, because editing something personal is always reluctant) that it didn't really go with this poem. It's good, but it needs a poem of its own. But because you are a wonderful audience, you got to read it here. Aren't you glad we have Deleted Lines?

- Megan

It's a Shame

Cheyenne

Its a shame she's a dream instead of a reality to him
but I guess dreams are something to be replaced once
you're done fantasizing
Falling in love with an idea of something better is much
easier to fall out of love with,
so she will blame herself, and see it as her own flaw
that she cant seem to be able to get her head out of the
clouds.
but what he didn't understand was it was his own firm
hands,
always grasping "brutal" in one fist, and "truth" in
another
that made her fall down and ruin her white dress,
ruin her fragile skin and cover her with bruises.

Some people say I love you in a different language made
of
broken bones and bleeding lips
because a fist is the only thing that will give their heart
the constant feeling of attention
sometimes being broken only feels complete when the
other persons objective
is to fix themselves by stripping what you have so they
have a reason to keep going.
He was draining her battery to charge his own faults.

Its a shame that shes an empty shell now,
because in that forbidden language of broken bones and
bleeding lips
he decided to take her heart, heavy like a loaded gun,
and shoot her.

Questions

Rhiannin

I'm forced to question.
At every turn
When it seems the answers should be so clear

Every time I hear all the same words
It scares me that the reactions have become
So cut and crystal clear

Why is it that each time I hear this utterance
It hurts not less but more
And I must in turn question

Why this response is ingrained I know not
Is it truly my fault? I can't know
If my actions are causes

Or if they are saying lies
Or if my ears are so tuned to the same repetition
That I see it where it lurks not

That my problems are petty
Or that my intentions are wrong
But most of all, that it is incorrect for me to

themselves deny.
And so I am forced to wonder only
Why?

My Brother Writes

Megan

My brother writes with Lego Bricks,
I ply my craft with words;
He thinks in cubes and cylinders,
I think in nouns and verbs.
He sees in three dimensions -
Up, down, left and right -
I see in two dimensions -
Black on paper white.
My thoughts spread ink across the page,
His build things up and out,
Images, we're both creating -
One in the mind, one out.
We each admire the other,
Envying their strength,
But if we ever had the choice,
We would not change, I think!

Commentary

This poem came to mind in September of 2011. My mom and I were discussing my brother's schoolwork. My brother and I are home-schooled, and my Mom was telling me about how she was watching my brother work on math. He kept staring into space and was moving very slowly, his mind clearly elsewhere. Finally, Mom said "You're thinking of a new Lego creation, aren't you?" He nodded, and she said "Well, go on up and build it then," knowing, as she confided to me, that they weren't going to get anywhere until it was out of his head.

As she described this to me, it struck me very suddenly that this was exactly how I was about writing stories - if I get a story in my head while working on schoolwork, I can't focus on anything until I get it down on paper - and I realized, with a bit of a jolt, that what my brother was doing was writing with his Lego bricks. That is, the thing I did with words was the same thing he did with plastic bricks. The need to express ourselves was the same, only the medium was different. Thus this poem was born.

- Megan

Summary

Megan Houghton

Part of growing up is figuring out who we are and who we want to be. We try to figure out what we believe in, and once we think we've figured it out, how do we tell others?

The pieces in this chapter remind us there are many ways to communicate, and as long as it is right for the individual, it is right. From creating physical things to combining words in order to make art, we all have a voice. And being able to get that voice out can consume our minds until it happens. Ink reminds us that often young people are ignored just as they're trying out their voice. It is our responsibility, as the generations guiding our youth, to support healthy confidence in their voices. We have to give them the chance to express themselves, and help encourage them to keep doing so.

On Society

We are all part of society, indeed many societies, from our neighborhood to the entire planet. More, we are active participants in those societies, or we should be. When they work, when they are positive and serve to build us all, we should celebrate. But when those societies fail us, we should raise our voices and get involved in the efforts to change and improve.

But, do we? Often we think that we can't make a difference, so why try. We leave it up to our leaders, somehow thinking it is their problem, but politics gets in the way. Or we simply "leave it to someone else," having too much on our plates with our daily lives. Still, once enough people do get involved, change does begin to happen.

At least that is the case for those of us who have reached the "age of majority" or more. People are willing to listen to our voices and consider what we have to say and what we do. But what of our youth? They experience the world and our societies, just as we do. And often they see more clearly without the fog of work and family responsibilities. But we rarely listen to their voices or consider their actions.

Take a few moments to put aside preconceived ideas and listen to what some of our youth tell us.

- Eric Smith

Power

George

Does power define the limit of me? People ask themselves this all the time. But, what does it mean to be powerful? You can say he or she is powerful but that doesn't make them any more capable of completing a task than you. If a person is working 2 jobs to support 4 kids, she is powerful; if you can wrestle an alligator then you are powerful; and if you can stand up to your superior without doubt or fear in your eyes, you are powerful.

Power is not going to come from someone else or from something; it has to come from within you. To get power you have to be fighting for something you believe in. You may get beat, but being powerful doesn't mean you win every time, it means that you try again until you do win. Power isn't always defined as fighting, sometimes it means being the support for someone else. Your own power can be used to give someone motivation, your power can give someone else their own power.

People who help others without recognition or compensation have power. People who don't let others dictate their lives and choices have power. People who will fight for someone they know little about, because it's the right thing to do, have power. People that possess power often don't think of themselves as having it. Any good leader in history has or had power, but often will be reluctant to talk about his own power. He may want more to reflect on the achievements of others he considers to have power.

Power can be misconceived. A car can be powerful. But, someone abusing their physical strength for their own personal gain is not power, it is selfish glory. Someone who is powerful doesn't need to get recognition for beating others to know they are powerful. If you have to see the look of terror or defeat in someone's eyes to feel like you have power, you are weak. Its easy to complain about a problem you have or someone you know has, but it takes a very powerful person to step into the judgmental view and help them without question.

Power is the will to support, to help others. If you have power you are willing to climb out of hell with another person. You will climb one inch at a time. You have no ignorance. You are without arrogance. When he looks you in the eye, he sees someone willing to sacrifice for him. Life is a game of inches. The inches someone needs are all around them; in people like you all around them. Don't underestimate your power. With your support, your power, someone can gain the inches that are the difference between winning and losing, between living and dying.

To have power is a blessing. Power is not the limit of your ability. Power is the ability you have to stand for something or someone you believe in and that you are willing to fight for to your last breath. This is what it means to have power.

Angry at the NSA (and everyone else who tracks my personal information)

Megan

The NSA has no right to monitor someone without reason. They have no right to monitor my personal phone calls and emails, to track me using my IP address or a GPS on my phone. I do not belong to them. This government belongs to me. The U.S. belongs to everyone, every citizen - that's what "We the People" means.

I have no problem with the NSA tracking people they suspect of being terrorists. I do object to them tracking my little brother, or my 11 year old cousin, who was thrilled to get her own email. NO ONE has the right to infringe on the rights of children or American citizens without good reason.

The founding fathers knew that this kind of "National Security paranoia" could happen. That's why the 4th amendment - a part of the inviolable Bill of Rights states "The right of the people to be SECURE in their PERSONS, HOUSES, PAPERS, and EFFECTS, SHALL NOT BE VIOLATED, and no Warrants shall issue BUT on PROBABLE CAUSE, supported by Oath or affirmation and particularly describing the place to be searched and the persons or things to be seized."

In other words, NO ONE, not the police nor the government, can look through my private stuff without "probable cause" and a warrant.

I know that doesn't mention internet. But the founding fathers didn't HAVE internet, did they? They just had private papers. Sadly, today many of our private papers are online. Where not only the NSA but many others can get at them. And that's what worries me.

Pollution

Brittney

We pollute the seas, the trees, the breeze.
We believe everything we're told,
and watch silently as humanity becomes a little too much for Earth to hold.
Some forget, and some were never taught that beauty rings
In everything
Instead of seeing and simply just being
We ignore all that is natural and lay down a shattered road
Humanity is slipping through the cracks that they forgot to patch
We live in the past.
The future is coming much too fast.
We see only what we want to see.
We choose not to believe
That the natural things we see
Are truly the key.

Generation

Rhiannin

Is it the fate of the generation
Rising to be the pride of the nation,
To be so easily mistaken
For statues of what that nation wants?

Girls and boys growing older,
In a world growing bolder,
Where freedom is the right of the people
With their voices constrained

Not by silence
But with the knowledge that in this world no matter
what
They say or they think,
Speak, shout, or sing,
No one will hear a damn thing
All of the sake of the power of age.
So scared to hear us, whether we're right or we're wrong.
If no one will listen?
How will we be strong?
For we're facing a world not faced
By the generations before,
How will we think feel and breathe,
This world we're left to,
If no one will see, that not you but we,

Must understand the perils this life brings.

Was it a mistake of our fathers, carried now long,
That says we must not speak out, it's wrong?
Were you listened to? The voice of your youth?
Were your ideas so strange?

Untamed?

Uncouth?

Why do you deny,
Your children fair true,
The faith of an ear,
A word of encouragement...
Two?

A Rant From a Pretty Opinionated Teen

Cheyenne

I am a teenager.
Given too many chances to become what society seeks,
but not enough to become what I wish to be
Taught at a young age that my body's my own, but when the world wants me, it can have me-
and I never asked for the opinion of anyone,
but when I start to doubt the worlds perspective on which direction we should be heading,
all of a sudden I become an X in a world of checks
✓ yes,
✗ no,
No became the word of the
Day,
Month,
Year,
The people around me contradicting each other- and confusing the shit out of me
Be hip, or don't be?
Smile for what you have, or cry for what you aren't doing for others in need?

Why can't I do both? Why can't I indulge in myself and still lend out a hand -
Societies become lower than I am - and I'm a 15 year old girl who apparently only thinks about sex.

Because, you know, I'm young, I can't apparently
"control my hormones" yet.

Why cant I go to school and openly sit with whoever I
want?
Why am I labeled a name but then forgotten as a
person?
this year I'm labeled a stoner, a drug addict, because of
how I dress
I'm sorry I didn't catch the memo that band shirts and
beanies mean I sell weed
And
I have never seen so many ignorant people.
Judging a black President for his skin, and not his
intentions
Do you even know about our past "white" Presidents?
I thought our generation would have been far over this.
I didn't know that hate still could run
so deep in the lives of the world's teens when it wasn't us
who lived in blindness,
but in the lives of our older inspirations
Why do our elders still teach hate in raw form-
and why do we find it's okay to listen to a singer
disrespect all races,
and women?
Think about your mom, your best friend, your sister.

We have wars trying to make this stop,

and yet when America wins a few, that gives us the right
to become to worlds police?
America, land of the free home of the brave -
I respect our troops,
but I don't respect the stupidity of what the governments
make them do
Fight for our freedom, not to take others away
I'm sick of seeing soldiers come home only to read their
obituary the next day.

I'm tired of seeing teens look at their wrists only to see a
painting of what they think is pain
I want you to look in the mirror, and see what I see
you're beautiful, but cries in the form are scars aren't
if you're sad, my ears are here to listen.
Listen to me - your weight doesn't define who you are
yes, being obese isn't healthy, but curves suite you quite
wonderfully
and guys, getting a little pussy isn't what you need
you're a teenager, find a best friend in her before you try
to unbutton her jeans

Women, we're strong, but we will never be equal to our
other sex.
We were made fragile, its just the curse of our curves,
no matter how tough we make our skin, our bones will
still bruise easily.

But we have brains, use them, don't abandon all
common sense
you don't need Photo Shop to look pretty,
you don't need makeup to fit the trend of today
Its a new year guys, it's time to wake the fuck up
Let me choose whether or not I love him, or her,
without being thrown into god's rage
I'm hoping 2014 will come with a new phase
one where we can all hold hands,
no matter of race, beliefs, sexism or pain
that way I can kiss her just the same way she kisses him
in the hallways

Its a new year, lets start it the right way.

Sons and Daughters

Rhiannin

Will my sons and daughters
Grow up in this world
Where nothing is a certainty,
And the constant
Changing values
Cause mass insanity.

For my sons I hope they grow up
In a world where
They can choose to be who
They be
And the pressures of society
Are not an all-compressing sea

For my daughters I hope they grow up
In a world where
They can reject the pressures
Of porcelain beauty
And be who they are inside
For all to see

I hope that my children
And my children's
Generational sibs
Do not live in a time

When both must hate the other
And a sister's best friend
Is also her worst enemy
When a brother's best friend
Is his foremost threat

Why in this world
Do we compete for
The right to be
Most abused.
Tote the challenges of the age
As the greatest accomplishments.

Men whose fortunes rival those of kingdoms
And women whose beauty surpasses fair Ophelia
Both caged to the fictional reality
And gender roles and duty.

I hope my children,
And my children's sibs
Never live with this ultimate uncertainty
Of never knowing, never seeing,
The truth
From the other point of view.

Leadership

George

This has been one of the worst weeks for me, but it has also been one of the best. Many people come to Big Horn. The participants come to learn leadership. The staff come to learn the impact of that leadership. Leadership is a force of nature. It will build an empire up or burn down a Kingdom. It is a gift bestowed upon those worthy of it, but it comes with a price.

If I have learned anything this week, leadership requires sacrifice. There has never been a monument built because of genocide or because of destruction. Monuments are made because of the sacrifice made in times of danger and destruction.

A good leader will tell you he worked for his power, a great leader will tell you he has done nothing but work for his people. It is not about how hard you can hit. It is about how hard you can fall and still stand after. Leadership without example isn't leadership, it is politics. If you pull someone up, then when you fall at your weakest, they will be there to pick you up.

Some believe power comes from destruction, but true power comes from compassion and forgiveness. So, after Big Horn, the next time you fall, standing will be made easier by the people you have lead to victory and suffered through failure with.

Big Horn (National Youth Leadership Training), Week 4, Troop Guide for Blue Patrol, 7/4/2013

Summary

David Romig

Society is too broad a topic for a book, let alone a chapter, but this chapter says a lot about the influence and pressures society places on our youth. Both of the works by George, "Power", and "Leadership", remind us that we have a responsibility to use our power and our leadership for the good of all of us. In particular, our youth, need support and encouragement to find and use their gifts of power and leadership for compassion and forgiveness, to move society in a more positive direction. All too often, we hear in the news about the misuse of power by those in leadership roles, mostly adults.

We hear about the abuse of power by the police. In The Washington Post dated Dec. 3, 2014 (Hinton, 2014) we see an article entitled "Mommy, why are police officers so bad?" Days later we read in another article that two police officers are killed in Brooklyn in an ambush by a young black adult (Mueller & Baker, 2014). Further, we are reading that more Americans view race as this country's most important issue. Cheyenne puts it well when she reminds us that President Obama is judged by his skin and not by his intentions. It may be that our youth have answers, and perhaps they have the willingness to make the needed sacrifices for positive change.

As Rhiannin shares, in "Generation", we "must understand the perils this life brings," as well as the mistakes we have made. It is time that we listen to our youth and hear their voices, for the future belongs to them. Their generation will determine the kind of world we will live in. If we cannot stop polluting, physically and socially, our planet, or as Brittney put it, our humanity will slip through the cracks. Then what kind of future and society will we have? Our world has many ills. We abuse, bully, and mistreat others, as well as our world. Our best hope for a better future lies with our youth; in their faith and determination to overcome what society has given them. Will they forgive us for what we have done and what we have failed to do? Can their compassion and forgiveness lead us to a brighter future? Rather than pressuring them with our preconceived ideas, we need to begin to listen to them. Only if we listen to our youth, and only if we are willing to change ourselves and how we interact with them, will we have the kind of future that we long and hope for. Will we listen?

It's Not A Challenge, If It's Easy

Eric Smith

When you started this book, we sought to challenge you, our reader, to take the time to actually listen to the Voices of our youth. But do they really have anything of value to say? Why should you listen? Consider, when you ask people who work with youth on a daily basis, you learn that young people are much smarter than society recognizes or accepts. Even then, many professionals don't really listen to what our youth try to tell us. They (indeed, most of us) get caught up in our "adult" mind set and close our thinking to only those insights from other adults, the recognized "experts." Can they really be experts if they don't seek insights from our youth, at least on issues affecting our youth? As a society, perhaps we think that our youth can't be wise precisely because they are young and inexperienced. After all, experience equates with wisdom, doesn't it?

If we equate experience with having greater knowledge, then it follows that very knowledgeable people must be wise (Ryan, 2013). Yet often the most knowledgeable people (think ivory tower academics or political pundits) lack the practical that is a hallmark of wisdom. In a sense, wisdom is applied, not simply spouted. Indeed, Ryan (2013) suggests that wisdom "requires practical knowledge about living." So, experience alone does not qualify as wisdom, and it is very possible for people with less experience to be wiser. Grant's (2013) simple definition, "Wisdom is the ability to make sound judgments and choices based on experience." clearly shows the connection.

Thus, simply equating wisdom with experience is not sufficient. In fact, the definition allows youth to be included among those who are considered wise, at least at times. Grant (2013) goes further, pointing out that there is no correlation between age and wisdom. It is not the amount of experience one has, but the application of thoughtful reflection to that experience. Even if we don't often see it, we must understand that our youth are very thoughtful and reflective, clearly demonstrated in the preceding chapters.

A second characteristic of wisdom, or at least insight, is how a person views the world. A rigid, black and white view does not result in wisdom. Instead, considering the subtleties, "shades of gray," leads to greater wisdom (Grant, 2013). It really means considering and balancing different views or aspects of experience, both that of others and our own. In the case of our youth, they are forming their world-views and, as a result, are often more flexible than older adults. Indeed, it is clear from many of the pieces in this collection that our youth do understand "shades of gray" and that wrestling with those shades is often where the greatest learning happens.

Wise people are characterized by a "willingness to challenge the status quo (Grant, 2013)." That is what our youth do while seeking their own identity, their own path and core beliefs, their own Voice. Indeed, we expect young people to challenge the ways and beliefs of their elders. It is part of adolescence. Sometimes the process results in misunderstanding our youth just when we expect them to grow and explore, leading to conflict. Perhaps listening to our youth as they push the boundaries would both smooth relationships and open our own eyes to alternatives. In fact, Grant (2013) suggests that wisdom comes from seeking to understand, rather than judge, a situation or a group of people. Again, as our youth challenge the norms and conventions around them, they seek to understand. Often they are much less judgmental than their parents, more accepting of individual choices and differences. Listening to their understanding or struggle to understand can be very instructive. It can result in interesting, sometimes significant insight.

Insight is the crux of this discussion. We can argue whether or not our youth may be wise. But, it is clear that they can, and often do, provide insight into situations as well as their own struggles. The value of that insight is improved understanding of our youth. And often, we gain improved understanding of ourselves. Consider, our youth are in many ways a reflection of ourselves, the bad as well as the good. We shape them to an extent. But we hope that our youth will rise above (or go beyond) that external "shaping" to find something more than we have achieved. It is what our extended adolescence is all about - growing, expanding, going beyond what we were given to create our own selves - Becoming.

Along the way, the struggles of our youth highlight both our triumphs and our faults. As they strive to forge their own paths as individuals, they reflect on what they experience and on the "shaping" we provide. The reflecting and integration they engage in (indeed, we all should) leads to improved insight and personal growth. But that growth can be inhibited. In fact, it often is. We don't really intend to slow them down, but when we fail to listen, *really listen*, to our youth, we do slow, perhaps even halt, their progress.

From this discussion, it is clear that there is reason to listen to our youth. And, having reached this point in the book, it is clear that you are listening. You have met the first challenge. *But, it isn't enough.*

We challenge you to do more than simply listen to the voices of our youth. They are simply words on a page, if you do nothing with them. Instead, we ask you to take the next step and ACT on what you have learned. It is simple to say, indeed, adults do it to each other as well as youth all the time - saying something will be done; but nothing happens. Instead, we ask you to let what you have learned either lead to direct action or inform your decision making processes and the actions you take when responding to situations affecting us all.

For example, we showed that even at preschool and elementary grades, our youth understand and follow a "code of silence?" What does that mean for our teachers and counselors when we want to work effectively with our youth? One approach is working to develop trust so that they are willing to forgo the silence in order to develop solutions to common problems in our culture, our society. That trust doesn't happen simply because an adult says "trust me," our youth need it demonstrated.

We showed that adults are often perceived as bullies. If you look at the bigotry and hatred many adults exhibit, and the way they treat each other in the workplace or on the playing field, it should be no surprise. But, our youth emulate that behavior, and at the same time they call us out for it. It is clear that we often don't understand how our actions are perceived - even well meaning adults often come across as bullies. When it is pointed out, they are horrified. They are not trying to bully, but adults often get carried away by the "mission" and don't see the accidental misunderstandings that happen when words and actions are not carefully considered. Worse, one of the consequences of our inattention is that our youth don't feel valued and will stop trying to reach across the years to share their insights. They may even come to resent us as they grow older, becoming what they resented as a youth. We must take action to change this pattern.

The preceding chapters show that our youth are smart, that they do think about their lives, positions in society, and what they would do, if they were positioned to change the world. They do understand what is wrong with our education system and they would like to help change it, if only they could get our attention. More, they do have insight into how their lives are shaped by their situations - health, economy, philosophy, even faith. They realize that bad, as well as good, things happen and it is the way each individual responds that determines the outcome for all.

Relationships are important to our youth, arguably more important than for adults. At the same time, they recognize that they are young and must gain experience and knowledge. Along with that recognition is the sense and the need to contribute - to share insights with those around them, if only we would listen. Sometimes those insights seem simplistic or trivial to the jaded adults listening. But are they? Recall the story of the little boy who said he wanted to "play with God." When examined carefully, with an open mind, it is profoundly wise. Yet, we rarely ask our youth for their insights. And even if we do, most often we don't really listen. Worse, we very rarely act on what we learn.

Think back to your youth. It was, most likely, rare that an adult genuinely asked your opinion. It did happen, but not much, even in school or church. Again, when we ask a young person for an opinion, how often do we actually pay attention to what he or she is telling us? Not often.

Our youth can and do give us insights into the things in society that trouble them, giving us an opportunity to engage and guide, both of which require action.

Our youth can and do try to tell us when bad things are happening so that we can intervene, though we often don't hear. When we do intervene (take action), we lessen youth stress, allowing healing.

Our youth can and do try to share their insights into the challenges we, as adults, face. But, we often don't hear those messages either. And when we do, do we include them in the solution?

We said earlier that listening is great, but not enough. What our youth ask, and deserve, is that we listen and take their insights and ideas to heart, then ACT. They are not asking us to agree with everything. But where we find value in their insights, they do ask that we make those insights part of our action plan. That is our challenge to you, our readers. Start with listening. Then **Do Something Positive** with the insights you have gained. We believe that if you have joined us on this journey of discovery, you have the strength to **ACT** on what you have learned through sharing with us. We recognize that it may not be easy to act. But, then, it wouldn't be a challenge if it was easy. Rise to the challenge and take the next step!

You Are Invited

We hope that you found something of value as you read this book. Perhaps you are inspired to share some of your own thoughts and feelings. This volume is, after all, only a beginning. We see this book and the volumes that follow as an opportunity for any young writer who so aspires to share her or his voice. To that end...

If you are a young writer, between the ages of 14 and 21, and you have something to say, we invite you to submit your work for possible inclusion in the next volume of Our Youth Speak.

Or, if you know a young writer, between the ages of 14 and 21, that might be interested, have them contact us.

Because we care about the integrity of our work and yours, if your work is selected for inclusion in the next volume, you will retain all ownership rights, licensing it for use in the book. You will be free to publish it anywhere you choose. Any works submitted, but not selected remain the property of their authors.

For any questions and to submit manuscripts, we can be reached by email at youthspeak@edglearning.com.

Thank you for being part of our journey.

The Writers of the Round Table

References

Donne, J (1624). Meditation 17. In *Devotions Upon Emergent Occasions.*

Grant, A. (2013). How to Think Like a Wise Person: Age and intelligence don't always bring better judgment; this does. *Psychology Today,* Retrieved October 31, 2014 from http://www.psychologytoday.com/blog/give-and-take/201308/how-think-wise-person

Gregory, D. (2009). Shame. Retrieved October 14, 2014 from http://www.lucifereffect.com/dehumanization.htm.

Hinton, J.F. (2014). Mommy, why are police officers so bad? *The Washington Post, December 3.* Retrieved December 23, 2014 from http://www.washingtonpost.com/news/parenting/wp/2014/12/03/mommy-why-are-police-officers-so-bad/

Mueller, B. & Baker, A. (2014). 2 N.Y.P.D. Officers Killed in Brooklyn Ambush; Suspect Commits Suicide. *The New York Times,* December 20. Retrieved December 23, 2014 from http://www.nytimes.com/2014/12/21/nyregion/two-police-officers-shot-in-their-patrol-car-in-brooklyn.html?_r=0.

Ryan, S. (2013). Wisdom. *Stanford Encyclopedia of Philosophy.* Retrieved October 31, 2014 from http://plato.stanford.edu/entries/wisdom/

Zimbardo, P. (2007). Dehumanizatioon, *The Lucifer Effect.* New York: Random House. Retrieved October 14, 2014 from http://www.lucifereffect.com/dehumanization.htm.

The Authors

Note: For our young writers, only first names are used. This is to help protect the minors in the group. If you would like to use any of their material, please contact permissions@edglearning.com. Adults contributing to this book will have their last names identified in these bios.

Brittney

I should have written my story as it was performed before my eyes. Perhaps, the story should have been written by my own hand before it was put on stage. But it appears that my hand was preoccupied in both cases. How was I to know that the details of my life were going to slowly slip away, leaving me only with bits and pieces to attempt to put together later on. More importantly, where was my mind when I was enacting in this play that is my life. So now as I try to piece together words to give you some perspective of who I am, I find that no great sum of words could ever portray exactly what we mean them to say.

So quite simply, my name is Brittney. I am 18 years old. And even though words hold no singular meaning, I hope you find some meaning in the words that are collected here.

Chad

Chad is a young man struggling to make his way in the kitchens of several different eateries. He is working to decide what he wants to do with his life before pursuing his higher education. He has a desire to help those around him, even when he can't manage to take care of himself. Laughter is known to make the best medicine. Chad tries his best to be generous with his humor, constantly attempting to provide the funniest antic he can supply to a situation. If antics are inappropriate, then Chad's love of education and science means he probably has some interesting fact to mention and discuss.

Cheyenne

Cheyenne hates writing biographies, and has avoided doing it for 3 months. She grew up writing about other, not herself, so she honestly really didn't want to write this- but for the sake of this book, she has begrudgingly sat down and decided to do it (Finally, three days after the due date). Cheyenne was born in a car, learned to write backwards before she could read from the left side of the page to the right, and was thinking of becoming a teacher but then realized she actually has a profound dislike for our current schooling system. An avid slam poet, she runs a literary arts club and has an extreme problem with "The Man"/any authority figure.

Cheyenne also comes off as an ass when she tries to be funny, but hey, stand up comedy was never her first career choice. She genuinely has enjoyed putting together every poem, and hopes you have just as much satisfaction reading every single piece as she had writing them.

David Benke

My daughter said, "Dad all your stories are about snakes or bugs."

I replied, "Sweetie, that's because they are about rural life in south Texas."

Of course it is also because many of life's lessons come by things stinging, biting, or sticking you. I used to tell my students a lot of stories to incorporate some life lessons in the math and only quit teaching when I realized that there seemed to be a curriculum based effort to make me boring. I believe, in 36 years they weren't able to pound it out of me, that teaching is about building a person not training for a test, and the most effective way that I knew to do that was through shared experience. Just remember all my stories are true or they should be.

David Romig

School had always been a struggle for David both academically and socially. He spent many nights working with his mother to help him with his learning. It was not until middle school that David could find lasting friendships with peers. As a result of his early difficulties and somewhat accidentally, David gained a passion for helping others. On a summer job, working as a teaching assistant with developmentally disabled students, David found a calling in his life. He completed his Bachelors of Science, a Master's degree in Applied Behavior Analysis, and then an Educational Specialist degree in School Psychology. David then found that he could use his skills and compassion to work with children who had many of the same kinds of struggles he had while growing up. By helping children, their parents, and their teachers he is able to make a positive difference in their lives. He hopes that this book may be another avenue for helping children to be heard, and helping the adults in their lives listen to them.

Eric Smith

While Eric has been a writer most of his professional life, the vast majority of that writing has been academic and technical for limited audience. This began to change with the release of his first cookbook, *George's Cookbook: Camping*. Now, Eric is the mentor/coach for the Writers of the Round Table. His journey to this position has been long and circuitous. He spent time as an editor of textbooks after college. At the same time he started coaching swimming, being a swimmer himself. Becoming frustrated with the textbook industry, where content was controlled not by the experts, but by the forces of the marketplace with politics sometimes overruling expertise, he went to graduate school to find a "better way." He found it in instructional design and educational technology. Along the way to a doctorate, he spent time coaching swimming with both youth and adults.

Eventually, he became a professor, then a consultant, and finally a teacher. Through it all, he combined his coaching skills with his instructional design training to develop effective learning experiences for his students. When his son expressed an interest in Cub Scouting, he returned to Scouting as an adult leader and trainer of other adults.

Eric's passion is to help young people learn, explore, and become more than they thought possible. He uses all of the skills and experiences gained along the way to support youth in their journeys, Indeed, the Writers of the Round Table was started to give young people desiring to explore and passionate about sharing their ideas through writing or other forms of media, to give them a Voice.

George

George has been reading and hearing stories since he was born. His father took great joy in reading to him every night for most of his early childhood. When he was in middle school and early high school he took an interest in entertainment. He loves telling jokes and stories to his friends, family, and others. Shortly after, he began creating his own films and even took a special class at school to learn more. The year after he took up interest in audio production. Entertaining and creating are big parts of George's life and his future as he see's it. Now he has to decide how to pursue those passions and ideals.

Megan

Megan has been telling stories since she was 2, and has been conducting scientific experiments almost as long – when she wasn't pretending she was teaching classes on TV. Given this strange but ever-present triune of loves, Megan has decided to pursue science in her academic life, while tutoring children and other students and continuing to write. She hopes to one day go to medical school, where she wants to become a doctor who works to solve her patients' problems, instead of shipping them off to another doctor who might or might not be able to help. She hopes to focus on the causes, effects, and treatments of food allergies, Multiple Chemical Sensitivity, and other understudied health issues. Megan has been homeschooled since the age of 5, an experience for which she is increasingly grateful.

Megan Houghton

Megan has spent years working with youth in a variety of ways. After high school, she worked with elementary students while working on her Special Education degree. While she loved watching the children learn and grow, she felt called in a different direction. Her passion is helping youth grow in character. She spends her time working with the Boy Scouts of America helping staff and Scouts. Megan was ecstatic with the chance to be a part of this book because she believes the youth need to be listened to.

Rhiannin

Rhiannin is in her second year of college, currently studying English and History. Her family will tell you that she has been telling stories almost from the time she could talk, and that her relatives soon learned not to let her start for fear of the words 'Chapter 2'. She hopes never to grow up, although growing older is inevitable. Dreaming of becoming a published author some day, she intends to write fantasy and historical fiction, although she is considering focusing on society today, and the problems facing western culture. With special interests in mental health, education, bullying, and the environment, she hopes to somehow effect positive change in these areas, although she is still trying to figure out ways to live out those goals.

Vlad

Vlad is a weird dude. He loves to cook and loves music. Vlad likes to help others. He also has a skill that most people find intelligent, he speaks three languages. He has studied culinary arts for one and half years. While studying, he was also working as a cook, which impeded on his home life. He is also there when his friends and family need him the most. For Vlad, close friends are family.